LO
WITH╵ ╵T
DUALITY

Awakening in Intimacy

B Prior

First Published in 2017

BERNIE PRIOR FOUNDATION LTD

30 Teddington Rd, Governors Bay,
RD1 Lyttelton, New Zealand

© The Bernie Prior Foundation 2017

"True union between man and woman is not for the faint hearted, nor is the knowing and living of eternal love.
It is for those rare ones who desire only their highest potential to realise God in their relatedness.
For they know that the highest calling will strip them naked of all their beliefs of a separate sensed self and leave them standing together in the transparency of realised Being; open and vulnerable, living a life of fullness and meaning."

Contents

In Conversation with Man

Interview On True Tantra

About B

Introduction

This book is a compilation of excerpts taken from talks and satsang with 'B' Prior, a Spiritual Master whose teaching on true partnership and higher sexuality are a bright light on the path of awakening in intimacy. The pieces spring from a profound and timeless conversation and enquiry into our original oneness nature and the profound meeting of mysteries that is 'man and woman'.

B's teaching is uniquely rooted in both Non-Duality and Tantra. He points to the one in all things, the 'One in the two' and the 'two in the One', and how an eternal and essentially incomprehensible union is manifest as our lives and as our sexuality.

The book encompasses both the highest vision and possibility for man and woman on this earth and the everyday living of it. B speaks of the pre-existing union of the Masculine and Feminine Principles, that they are not two, but are one; Awareness-Knowing, Oneness moving or the 'I Am'.

His conveyance of this is unique and does not match current molds of how we have come to understand and engage the Masculine and Feminine, as expressed in colloquial phrases such as: "I am getting in touch with my inner feminine." or "I am developing my inner masculine." or " His feminine and my masculine side hit it off perfectly."

B's invitation is into an entirely different frequency and frequency of embodiment – the realisation, beyond any concept, that the eternal dance of form and formlessness, of Consciousness and Awareness, is not exterior but is essentially what we are as Source-Being. Anything we could possibly perceive in our senses is the union of the principles in movement as all things and *this* is pure sexuality.

'Love Without Duality' reveals the possibility of a true way of relating as one, wholeness to wholeness, the Beloved to the Beloved. It evokes deep reading and subtle listening and right there, the heart already knows its highest possibility: Self-realisation.

The writing is kept in line with B's verbal style to fully maintain the essence and transmission of his teaching. The flow of the chapters develops vertically, from the highest downwards, opening with subtle, abstract pieces and ending in down to earth and intimate dialogues about life in deepening partnership.

B speaks as Awareness to Awareness, Being to Being. His words arise in and address within the listener the immeasurable reality one is.

You will find that there is a silent transmission in the words that transcends the mental realm. In reading, be still, go slow, open and allow the words to permeate, percolate, awaken and ignite the sparks of your own heart's knowing.

The Highest Possibility: Realisation

"In the manifest universe, all that truly exists is the union of the profound Masculine and Feminine moved in One Self, one body. To discover this in your relating within, to discover the other is within you, and be awakened in two bodies is the kind of enlightenment most people have no idea about."

1

Two Realising The One

"It is possible for an apparent two to realise the One, to love the Beloved in another, in man and woman and realise union beyond all space and time. This is a rare realisation."

Mostly we think of enlightenment as happening in a singular entity or individual, but there is also an entirely different realisation that is still very rare on earth: to awaken to man and woman as one being, one moving evolution of the life of this planet, appearing through what seems to be two bodies and two utterly different possibilities. It *is* possible for man and woman to be so one that they transcend all space and time and in that know one goodness, one God-ness, one love, one utter realisation with no beginning or end.

This will utterly change not only how man sees himself and woman sees herself, but change their purpose to ever be with another, for there is no self-orientation in this. There is nothing to *gain* for a self, only to *give up* the self to the greater calling to unify in love and in the making of love. Whether they physically make love together or make it in the unseen, love will be known and literally 'made' in these bodies.

That is the possibility. Should this become realised in their relationship together, they will know that this union is not actually *of* this planet. It is beyond all space and all time, moves beyond all space and time and yet floods all space and all time.

Even great realisers rarely speak of this possibility, of the realisation of the Masculine and Feminine Principles within bodies that will pass away, for God to behold God in Masculine and Feminine Consciousness. Where He and She come through and merge, they are not the self seen in the bathroom mirror. They are the pure light of Consciousness moving in union creating the manifest universe. They come from beyond the stars yet they form and move the planets and the stars. They seek intelligent forms of man and woman through whom they could for one moment alone have conscious form of true love's meeting.

This *can* be realised between man and woman who begin to see and know deeply, who discern through pure love and the deep engagement of their knowing inside. There is a marriage, a merging where all they know is 'no other.' Egoity is simply seen to be false, an illusion. There has never been two. 'I' has always been One. It is a relationship that is infinitely deeper than their body-mind identity, even deeper than this earth. *This* is what this earth is for.

2

Ways To God

*"We are destined to become one body,
destined to realise one consciousness in all bodies."*

There are many ways to God. I am going to point to two and
then I will speak about another, which is 'my way'. The first
way says: "Nothing outside of you is real. Only the
Consciousness that is seeing the objects is real. I, who am
seeing and knowing, am That, free of all forms." This is
You, the 'I Am' that does not pass away.

There is experience Now and that experience will pass away.
What never passes away is the knower of all experience who
is beyond all experience. It is the 'I Am'. The 'I Am'
remains beyond experience. It is unaffected by what
constantly passes away. 'I Am' is the only place that you can
say is constantly real.

You can realise the Self by looking at a wall, seeing through
and emptying out the content of your consciousness. You
can realise That which does not pass away. That is the
Masculine - the realisation of God through no-thing is the
Masculine realm.

The second way says: "Everything that could possibly exist
is What I Am. Everything that ever happens in existence,
without exception - good, bad or ugly is What I Am. I am the
constant movement and change of all things. I am the All. I
am every-thing."

In fully embracing all movement, you can realise beyond your body-mind identity that you are love. That is the Feminine - the realisation of God through all that is, is the Feminine realm.

What I see as 'my way' puts the two ways together. The union of the two, the Masculine and Feminine is the adventure of the universe. This is tantra.

I am no-thing and I am every-thing. I am everything yet I am the Pure Consciousness that pervades everything as nothing. I am free of all movement, free of all energy, free of all forms and free of all experience. I am That as nothing and I am everything that moves. I am everything that flowers. I am every planet, every star, every drop of water, every mountain, every tree, everyone, both in the senses and in the finest tip of golden light. I am That.

In this synthesis, a real human being is born, one who is evolving in a profound and vertical way of consciousness, coming from nowhere and going to nowhere, yet with profound direction and vision in this human life. This is the destiny of every man and woman, to evolve consciousness, to evolve relationship, to evolve humanity.

*The Calling
to Unify in Love*

*"I am speaking about the deep calling
to know man, to know woman intimately
as Being embodied as man and woman,
to know God or Source with no beginning and end
in the depth of the Consciousness of what man is
and in the depth and opening of
what woman is as the light of love
with no beginning, no end and no self."*

3

Mystical Love Evolves The Universe

"Be called to a love that is greater than your self and the earth will reveal its treasures. The entire universe is wooed open in a true calling to love."

The calling of man and woman is a powerful sacred domain of transformation. It is the real possibility of flowering the heart, opening and clearing the mind and discovering a mystical love in our union. This begins to cleanse and heal, not only the man, the woman and the partnership, but cleanse and heal our societies, our culture, our earth. We have incredible power hidden asleep within us as man and woman. The invitation of a real calling is to discover this power, to unlock it and create with it a new human being, a new radiant life on earth.

To be authentic, to be able to access reality as our home and to bring from reality greater potential into our life doesn't happen when we don't see that there is a sacred purpose in the pull of man and woman. The light of this calling comes from a profound place within. It is entirely involved in evolving humanity to higher and higher places of love and participation in the universe.

We have such capacity inside ourselves but when it is sleeping in self-concern, we create painful suffering relationships and painful limited societies. At core, every man and woman is the Authentic Self that creates the universe. We can be authentically our Self, the 'I' that was not born, the 'I' that will not die, the 'I' that has always been here since before time, the 'I' that transcends all time and all space.

This must be at the core of our heart and our knowledge in all perceived activity. We must be That and no matter what moves within, remain authentic and one hundred percent engaged with 'What Is'.

To be our Self is to be completely and absolutely aligned with the light of Pure Being and engage all forms of life as they are. If we pull out just one percent of 'what is', we begin to weave a web of self-deceit.

We have an untold ability to transform the world of form and to bring an integral relationship of what we are in the deep, into our interior, into the person. The person becomes the vehicle that unites the interior and the Absolute with the environment, the individual and the All.

4

The Greater Mystery

"Both man and woman have forgotten who they are; that they are the divine principles that the entire universe manifests from. They think they are men and women but they are profound Consciousness in divine Form in union already, moving the universe, evolving Consciousness and its forms."

I am pointing to a greater mystery than man and woman as selves. I am saying that in both man and woman there is more than just 'man and woman'. The universe knows itself through your union and your loving. You can know the universe, know and realise the creator, know and realise the Self, through your unfamiliar movement towards one another.

When you end your familiarity, and stay open to meet each other not using your past or any form of self-identification, you unfold your knowing, which is the light of your heart. As you reach into the deep of each other, you reveal the greater realities hidden in woman's body, which is far deeper than the flesh and hidden in man, in the depth of the Consciousness that he is. When you open to deeper reality and that reality is brought into a relationship with your self, your self changes. This is tantra or the love of God through the calling of man and woman. Such love utterly changes life.

If your self and life don't change, you are living an old paradigm. You are not living the fullness of deeper realisation together where there is the dance of 'two as One' and all that this opens in your human sphere of the universe and of the mystery.

5

The Play Of Consciousness And Awareness

"Your calling is the draw to the realisation of your unity, to completely marry and dissolve in the apparent opposite force of Masculine and Feminine power, energy and consciousness. That is oneness."

Your calling is to realise deeper than the placeless place you came out of. No matter what takes place in life, even in pain and suffering, there is a deeper level you are being called to, a level deep in the beyond which I call the unseen You, a level deeper in the body yet to manifest. It is the meeting of what is deep in the beyond and what is deep in the body. This actually gets played out between man and woman.

Man and woman are the play of Consciousness and Awareness with the divine purpose to bring the principles of the universe, the Masculine and Feminine that spill out of and flow from the Real Self, into embodiment.

When man and woman fully respond to what is deeper than their separate sense of self, which I locate as 'Awareness-Knowing at the heart', they open deeper levels of their profundity in their body and transcendentally, which means in their consciousness. They awaken in the depth of a body that transcends the bathroom mirror. They awaken in a knowing that transcends their separate sense of self.

6

True Union - A Calling Beyond Attraction

"The Masculine and Feminine calling is the only real attraction in the universe, it is the pull to Source or pure love that already is One. The two already are One and their calling is to embody that oneness in two-ness, as one universal body."

True union is not for your self. It is for the meeting of what you really are in the deep of you. It is a calling. It is beyond attraction because attraction has duality in it - likes and dislikes. A calling is when your being calls for that that is truly deep.

A calling could be that the one you are called to is nothing like your self would want him or her to be. When you really awaken to a calling, there is no aversion. Attraction implies aversion, there will be opposites. In a true calling, although there is still attraction and aversion in your psyche, you begin to align your heart; you are knowing the deep with all your forms of relating, seeing and belonging. Although opposites come up, they are met by your union and aversion is transcended.

When you are really called into deeper intimacy, your life is no longer yours as a separate sense of self to the other. Your life belongs to truth. There is a marriage in your heart, in your being, in your body with the apparent other. The other disappears because you are meeting inside and you see and experience clearly there is no other in the true meeting of love. In that moment, you are one and your oneness is not a subject-object relationship. It is a totality, a complete immersion into the profound.

7

The End Of Linear Man And Woman

"When you are really called into deeper intimacy,
your life is no longer yours as a separate sense of self.
Your life belongs to truth.
There is no 'other' in the true meeting of love."

There is no such thing as a man and woman when the light of love that I am speaking of is met. When love's light meets, it is the end of man and woman. There is no man and woman. There is profoundly masculine consciousness that pervades the universe and has nothing in it and there is the feminine consciousness of all that is, the light of love, multi-dimensional forms of love. She is everywhere.

When man and woman are attracted and it is a true calling, this moment is the end of a linear man or woman. The immediacy of love's light is all pervading stillness and consciousness.

I-man, I-woman am That in a single moment.
I am in the experience of totality in a single flash.

That is why it is so beautiful, so attractive and freeing because you have been freed of being a man or a woman. You are the eternal Consciousness of the Masculine and Feminine. You are free.

8

The Mysteries That Pass Between Man and Woman

"The mysteries that pass between man and woman are sublime. They do not belong to a separate sense of self and yet you can awaken and you can say: God, You so opened me!"

When man and woman first meet each other, they are knowing the mystery of each other. They are knowing the light that is shining in form.

When he first sees her, it is a real opening in the deep. He knows he knows her because she is already one with him inside, his other half, the other half of his Godhood, the manifest half of light and energy moving and manifesting forms of creation through the love of the One.

There is a mystery behind this. He wants to enter that mystery but to really enter it he will have to come towards her. He sees the mystery in her and he wants to kiss that mystery. He wants to hold the hands of that mystery, really go right into that mystery. That mystery has a guardian though. In fact, there are many guardians of her mystery. To come into the mystery of woman, man has to have a finer consciousness, a finer presence to reach into her deeper garden. To reach into her real mystery, he will pay the price of entering so deeply. That price will be his separate sensed self, the belief that he is a body-mind. In truth, He is Consciousness. His form is actually Her form. She is manifesting his body.

He will have to come into her body and feel it all, so he will have to incarnate and not stay aloof from all that she experiences, all that she feels on every level. He will have to come right in and that will cost him all of his self. He will need to stay in the right direction to come into her mystery and that will reveal his mystery.

In the same way, when woman beholds man and she knows him with her heart and that knowing fills her body, she is knowing Him in the deep of her beyond her embodiment and he is knowing Her with his embodiment. For her to know his mystery, she is going to be called to dissolve her relationship with her past, her relationship with her old forms, as he also has to dissolve his relationship with his old direction, his old consciousness.

The light they saw in each other will remake their forms and awaken new consciousness in both of them; an entirely new beingness of the Feminine and the Masculine creates a new movement and a new form of consciousness appearing as man and woman, walking as one body, one life in profound intimacy. That changes how they experience their lovemaking, their life and what they relate to.

Everything gets to change when they are meeting this deep. When man and woman go through all the change, they have to go through it consciously awake to what called them to dare to kiss each other, to dare to be together.

Their mystery will open. He will be able to speak of her mystery. His love for her will come through his fingers, come through his eyes, come through his life, come through the adoration of her. Just a look from him and she will come on fire with his knowing Her in the deepest place.

In the opening of his knowing of Her and her knowing of Him, her body changes and re-forms an entirely new kind of woman. The mystery of woman begins to be embodied through her lips, through her feet, through the smallest movement of her body and her life. She begins to form her mystery. It is not something that she is doing, it is because she is being met and known in the deep and that gives her access to his new consciousness. She begins to mirror his new consciousness, his new possibility, his mystery.

Bringing this into the world is the whole meaning of their love, to unite the beyond in the manifest and the manifest in the beyond. This is why man and woman walk together, dare to kiss and dare to make love. They are really called to making God together.

The Universe Is
Pure Sexuality

*"Pure sexuality is the means in which
we commune with all of life, with a bird, a river,
a mountain, an ocean, a star and with an other.
We commune with our bodies with that that is in
manifestation. In this, we become intimately connected with
the whole field of universal life.*

*In intimate sexual union, in the pure intimacy of Being,
two people can unite their being and their bodies
as one whole sphere of life and Consciousness.
The seen and the unseen become known, experienced and
expressed in true intimate sexuality. The realisation of God
is contained within this union, contained within their
meeting as One Being embodied."*

9

How Much Do You Really Know About Sexuality?

*"So much more than mere sexuality is hidden within the pull
of intimacy. It holds the innermost secrets of the universe."*

How much do you really know about sexuality? How much
do you really know? How much does the word
'sexuality' either close you down or open you up in
excitement? Neither the closure nor the opening is a true
understanding. Sexuality isn't just situated in the genital
area. Sexuality is the purity of love moving as energy, the
purity of light moving, having Awareness, Consciousness
and immediate real form. Sexuality is Now.

Sexuality belongs to an incredible span of divine
Consciousness that is what you are. You don't *have*
sexuality, you *are* it. You create the universe as you give
expression to what you are right now as pure sexual energy
that manifests light into forms of expression. Your calling in
your entire life, not just with a man or a woman, is to give
expression as the pure heart to all that you are opening into
in the mystical you, the innermost you.

In truth, you have done it already; it's called the universe. It
is constantly changing like the cells of your body and your
relationships. It cannot stop changing. It cannot stop ending.
It cannot stop knowing increasingly deeper for there is no
end to what one can be and bring into life. There is no end to
your heart and your way home in the expression of your life.
This is your pure sexual energy, one with the light of

primal Consciousness, instantly making everything that you know and behold, right now.

10

When Being Moves Your Sexuality

"When Awareness moves from the heart of Being, sexuality follows Being and Being follows sexuality. This is the merging of Being and sexuality which is the movement of love."

The entire manifest universe is really a movement of Pure Being flowing through pure sexuality. The universe is the pure making of love. When your being moves your sexuality, that is the highest frequency of real life.

If you didn't have sexuality, you wouldn't be able to know what a flower is, what a tree is, what the sky is. These are higher levels of sexuality where you know the beingness of the universe, of an animal, of a flower, of a mountain with your body and your heart. That is a movement of pure sexuality known in your being.

When Being moves your sexuality, it is pure and when pure sexuality moves, your being opens in utter purity. When your self moves your sexual field, it is not pure. It is of and for a separate sense of self. We are not taught what sexuality really is and that we are actually born into a pure sexual field moved and inspired by the profound beingness that both is and knows the universe.

11

A Flow Of Oneness

"There can be no oneness of humanity unless man and woman are deeply knowing and embodying each other on every level of their life together. The moment you make 'other' is the moment you make Duality."

Oneness is a flow of true sexuality. Oneness is a level of intimacy that includes all of you, every aspect of you in communion. You whole-bodily merge in the heart and every cell in the body comes alive as one love.

True sexuality is your entire body opened to your heart. There is no subject or object. This is why in realisation you can have whole body experience with the divine. You may have heard of nuns saying that Jesus made love to them for instance. It is utterly possible, because to be in deep communion with Christ or Pure Consciousness, the whole body opens and in that moment the body is divined in the grace of love. This is far too intimate for most humans because humanity at the moment practices separation. We make ourselves separate bodies with separate sensed experience.

12

The Union Of Awareness-Knowing

"Movement is sexuality. Deep Sexuality is how the entire cosmos moves. Deep Sexuality is the movement of oneness moving all forms, from light to energy to physical form."

All movement is a sexual movement. There is nothing that is not sexuality moving. Life is sexuality moving. The entire universe is the union of Awareness-Knowing. Awareness-Knowing moves the universe and as it moves, in an instant just beyond the movement, there are the Masculine and Feminine Principles that are one in Real Self and this union is expressed. It is the goodness that is in the entire cosmos.

Anything you do whilst you as Awareness have a body involves sexuality. When it belongs to your self-experience, then it is a very shallow movement. It is about your self. You are defining your self through sexual experience but sexual experience cannot define what you are as Awareness-Knowing.

Sexuality split from your heart is a distortion of your consciousness and your relationships then distort. They become about 'a me'.

When movement is known from the heart then sexuality belongs to the heart. Your sexuality or your formed life and its movement aligned with what you are knowing in your heart is the beginning of the Real You. The Real You will start to form in your relationships.

When we are called to another in deeper intimacy, it is not actually about something for the self. It is about a union of Being that then fills the heart, fills the body and fills the self with what love really is. When two are moving in that way, there is such a deepening and such an opening, it cannot be missed. It has nothing to do with your self. Nothing whatsoever.

Sexuality Given Back To Your Heart

"Profound sexuality is the radiance of the heart, the one and only moment of creation. Everything else is second to that moment."

The energetics of nature on the planet are designed to keep the bodies being made. There is a mechanism within the psyche of the earth that moves all creatures to procreate. Nature conspires not to just pro-create but to create true forms of 'Being I-Aware', all in the profound blueprint of the universal design for any star system and planetary consciousness.

When you raise up your sexuality beyond just the need of sex, you begin to see that the energetics of the whole planetary structure is pure sexuality and moving through that pure sexuality is the light of Being. That is love.

Sexuality and light moving through is the making of real Consciousness having real intelligent forms. It is the movement of love that enables you to know love in all things, all at the level of your heart, like a radiating sun filling up your heart that knows all forms are the formulation of that union.

Whilst you as Awareness move sexually from patterns, parental or societal or the need for experience, you soon discover that the root chakra is not a function of its own, it is actually a function of the heart and Being, a radiance of Pure

Self shining. It is also a point within the brain that is totally connected with the cosmic movement of all life streaming bright-full Awareness-Knowing, forming a greater reality all the way into this denser form.

When you have had enough sexual experience, you discover that sex on its own is not fulfilling and ties you to the body-mind and its attachments. It doesn't give you the ability to profoundly be with anything in the universe and know its profundity, its love, its grace, its wonder and its mystery.

When your sexuality is really coming forth from your heart, you are enabled to read the mystery of the earth and the universe and the mystery of another with whom you have a calling to know love. This is a transmission of beingness that has all the forms of your life. You are able to move deeply into this life and into union with God in another, with the divine in another.

Sex not given to your heart builds fears and creates suffering. You then attach emotion to the fear and suffering and to your forms and they will not let you open to what love really is in your body with another or even with a flower.

In giving your sexuality back to your heart, to the truth within you, all your old sex will empty out of your body to reveal what love is in the body. Old sexuality will definitely come out and trigger every level of emotion possible, every level of mental distortion possible and all this is known in your body and in your sexuality.

You will need to awaken in that by leaving all that alone and awaken to your heart. You will come upon heartbreak you didn't even remember you had because you buried it so deep. It is good that you come upon heartbreak, so you can release the energy back to your heart.

Now for you this is no problem, for you are knowing with your being what sexuality really is. It is singing in the birds, moving in the skies, it is in all creatures and in all things. That is a movement of love and it always opens up the deep.

Pure Divine Principles

*"Man and Woman are bound by time.
The Masculine and Feminine are timeless. They are infinite.
They are the divine intelligence of One Self. They seek each
other in the bodies of man and woman so their light can
merge and come all the way through into form."*

14

Pure Consciousness And Pure Form

"He is the formless experience of Consciousness.
He is the deep.
She is the display as the entire cosmos of the deep.
She is the body of the deep. She is Now.
She has no beginning and no end as She gives form to the
formless."

The Feminine and Masculine Principles are not two, they are already One. They are already Here. The stars shine because of their union, life manifests because of their union and the intelligence of this relationship is love.

He, The Masculine Principle

The Masculine is Pure Consciousness, pure space that has profound direction. He, not man, is that that moves from nowhere, going nowhere. In that action or direction, all the forms of relationship evolve to realise the Self.

The Masculine is a vertical reality. Masculine Consciousness is vertical. In that verticality, life moves and evolves. It has no past as a pattern or programming that has a future. It is vertical, always Here, present Now, the one and only reality this very instant. There is no past and yet it is filled with pure potential, which could be called its future. It has never existed before, for it only exists Now.

She, The Feminine Principle

She is all phenomena, all forms of life. She is the entire sexual energetic field of the manifest universe. She is pure sexual energy expressed from the heart of Source. This equates to love.

The real She is radiantly free. She is the light of Consciousness as the Feminine Principle. She is the expression of beingness already in union with the beingness of the Masculine. She is the formed movement of love.

She is the love that relates all forms of beingness to the One. She loves that One because it is Him in his seat of the deep, one with Her. She relates form. That's why she loves relationships. She relates form to her deepest knowing. She relates all the forms only to the One. She doesn't relate them to any sense of self or person for She has none. She is the light of love herself. She relates everything to the divine.

This is her potential. That makes her forms of relationship pure. She is the pure relatedness of the Feminine Principle. She knows it all belongs to the One, the Great Being, from which She springs forth.

15

Joining In The Authentic Self

*"The evolution of humanity as universal beings arrives in
the discovery of true intimacy on this earth."*

The Masculine is a profound shaft of light. This is He. You
could say, He is 'Phallus', a shaft of light, coming from
nowhere, going to nowhere. Endless. He is a pillar of
profound No-thing-light. There is nothing in it, just pure,
awesome, penetrative Consciousness.

Around Him spins the spiral of the Feminine. The Feminine
joins the shaft of light. Where they join is the Authentic Self.
The place where they join is where She is real, He is real,
where they are one reality.

She spirals in ever increasingly larger circles around the
shaft of light until She gives birth to Her Self as you and I.

At the highest point, the spiral is profoundly, purely
Feminine. That is what I call 'She'. She is all that could
possibly ever be in all space, all time and all form. She is the
fullest of potential, the fullest of light. She, in that place, is
the principle of love. She is 'all that is'.

She also spirals down the shaft and in that way, the light that
She is has the potential of embodying what She is as the
profundity of endless love and loving. It moves all the way
down on each sphere of manifest existence. Up at the top,
She is just one little dot beginning to spiral. Down at the

bottom of the spiral, She is enormous. She is actually biggest in her smallest part and smallest in her biggest part. Down at the bottom, She is woman. Up at the top, She is the Feminine. She is the potentiality in every woman in every sphere of life.

She has embodied. She has spun the web of form. She has given man a body. The shaft of light on a man's body and the spiral in a woman's body are the phallus and the yoni. The shaft of light engages the spiral. Each level of the spiral is a level of where the Feminine is as woman.

I could say, "Woman, where are you on the spiral? Man, see where your creative energy is on the spiral? Where are you in the shaft?"

16

The One In The All And The All In The One

"She is about relationship. She wants to care for all - all relationships, and bring them to the One. He is about the One, He cares for the One in the All. She cares for the All in the One.

He is the relationship of the One in the All. It is entirely different. He is one-pointed, which raises Her care higher and higher. He brings it into verticality. She spirals it round and round, up and up."

The divine Feminine is not the Mother. She is the prior state of Mother. He, the Masculine Principle, is the prior state of Father. Before they move, the divine Feminine is all that is. She is 'what is'. She is total aloneness, just as He is total aloneness yet they are one, all-oneness.

The moment they move, the divine Feminine relates what She is to all the forms of the universe. That is when She turns into the divine Mother being what She is as She spirals around the universe that is spilling out of Her belly.

She becomes what She is in her radiance and relates that to what She is as the Mother. The Mother is the relationship aspect. She is raising every being back into the higher room of Her belly, to relate all those forms to the axis, Pure Consciousness, the Father. In that relationship, all forms spiral around the axis, all forms know the axis and the axis knows all the forms. They disappear into oneness.

17

A Movement of Infinity

"Man and woman are endlessly evolving and raising up the deep to the surface and returning the surface to the deep. That's the calling of man and woman. The goldenness they experience in each other is not the man-form or the woman-form. The goldenness they experience is beyond form."

In truth, man and woman are the divine principles of the Godhead. It is not 'man and woman' that are pulled together, this is on a lower level of human experience. What is really drawn in the calling between man and woman is the Masculine and the Feminine Principles that already are one Consciousness.

The Feminine Principle is form and energy equaling love and the Masculine Principle is profound Consciousness, Awareness and direction.

It is like in the infinity symbol, where form runs into the unseen Consciousness and the unseen Consciousness runs into form, a flow of Consciousness that is neither form nor formlessness. It is one and it can be experienced in a relationship as God in love with itself as man and woman.

This is the descending of Godhood as the Masculine Principle and the Feminine Principle into the human heart, uniting a man and a woman together at the core. This is the supreme love we are all destined to experience and integrate in our human life.

In truth, this is all that is happening, yet it seems to be the hardest thing to unite man and woman at core where they are no longer separate selves but one Being, one love.

18

Masculine and Feminine Power - Man and Woman

"Man represents the Consciousness half of the One. He sees as Consciousness, She sees as relationship to forms, two different ways of seeing. Without this there wouldn't be the life that we experience. Without this connection of the two who are already one, neither the formless realm of Being nor the formed realm of Becoming would be in relationship."

I see masculine power as true nobody-ness or emptiness. I see man as the innermost consciousness where nothing is going on from the sense perception point of view. It often disturbs woman because man can be quite empty and there are those times when he doesn't want to have anything to do with all the movement. It is a power of no-thing that is indescribable. Man doesn't know what that power is. He doesn't know it without the connection to woman. It is her that awakens who He is, just as it is him who awakens who She is.

His power or His home is an innermost emptiness that is full of levels of beingness that do not yet have any form. It is a formless place, a dimension of beingness that has no form yet is destined to have form so it can know what it is in reflection.

Man in his deeper place, knows the direction of his life and of his intimacy with woman is to bring down that formless place and to energise it into form by being that in the presence of this manifest universe. It becomes apparent that He is actually not of this universe but of another place.

Woman often doesn't understand him but when he sees her with all his heart through the light that shines in his eyes, she knows who He is. Even though she cannot describe Him, she knows she wants to be with Him.

It is a directive flow of endless power that actually doesn't have power *over* anything or a need to have anything. That is a true man. When a man truly loves woman, he doesn't control her. In him just being with her, she feels met, held, known and healed. She feels everything that is good, the goodness of being together. He is the power that truly knows the direction of life and it is not of his man-self, it is of his divinity.

The Feminine or She gives immediate expression to what emptiness is. She is the light, the power and the energy of all the forms we experience. The highest Feminine Principle contains every possible form there is. She is in relationship with every being in form throughout the entire cosmos. She is the body-mind-womb in which the entire cosmos has life.

She relates. She is beautifully in relationship with all Being. She is the master of relationship and woman has the ability to either create new forms in her connection with her divinity or to hold old forms together and keep them the same.

Which does she want to be? Does she want to be giving new forms to her innermost love or is she holding onto the past believing that she needs the security of the past forms? It is truly up to her whether she wants to be the vast Feminine which is her true power or remain contained in her 'little personal life', keeping herself a separate woman.

In truth, we can relate this to both man and woman. Both can choose to keep their separate lives going, using their self to remember the past in terms of positive and negative experience. In that way, they are always recycling the past, trying to avoid the bad and to re-stimulate the good. That is the illusion they live in, one that is not of the cosmos but of their own separate mind, their own separate sense of self.

They can belong to the greater Masculine and Feminine that are the Father and the Mother, the principles of oneness that are constantly attuned to the more, the full potential that has not yet had life and calls to have form. In their deepest place, man and woman give birth to the new children of the universe, which spill out of their loving together. Ever-new, ever deeper no-place places begin to have form through man and woman's divine connection, communion and loving. They bring in the more. That that has not yet had existence can come through the life and the genuine connection and union of the Masculine and Feminine heart as oneness.

That is what we are here for. We are not here to keep each other the same. We come together to change each other, not from self but from our divine connection, communion and knowledge.

It is our love that brings more in. If we truly are eternal, real love will change all the images of our belonging. We will begin to be in the divine passion of experiencing more and more of our love connection having more and more form.

That is true abundance, not just abundance of form in terms of physical form but of every aspect of what our divine intelligence is, in light, in energy, in the unseen, in the human psyche and finally in form. We are the bringers of light into form.

The love of a man and a woman truly divinely connecting sends out a wave of a love-field that changes those around them. People begin to recognise their True Self and to live the more of what they are. The world will change through this kind of loving.

This is the power of true hearts. No matter what goes on in the process of that union coming together, we are re-mastering the universe, re-mastering the body-mind. We are recreating our humanness in the likeness of the Real Self.

This is the communication and the frequency that moves as we move, whether we move a finger, whether we move our body or move into true feeling. It is a transmission. This is what this planet needs. It needs the living transmission of love, which is the union of every man and every woman's heart within their own self and within each other.

19

The Dark Feminine

"The gift of the real Feminine in both her nature as light and her nature as the dark is fire. Fire is her gift, the fire of transformation."

Everyone speaks of the arising of the Goddess or the pure Feminine. To arrive at the arising of the Goddess, you have to realise that She comes through the meeting of the Dark Feminine. You have to meet the Dark Feminine for the pure Feminine to have space, for the pure Feminine to have her real face and form.

The Dark Feminine is what purifies the past, your concept of who you are and how you relate to whom and to what. You cannot discount the Dark Feminine. She has to be met wherever She shows up.

The Dark Feminine isn't just in woman but also in man and in the world. By meeting the Dark Feminine, the pure Feminine, which is always Now, comes fully alive in your knowing, in your seeing and in your experience.

20

Shedding The Sheaths

"We have to be on our knees and bow down in our hearts to all other hearts and to every life experience, not as weak, feeble individuals, but as primal Consciousness, as that that we truly are."

Man is a shaft of light in his deepest place. Woman is a spiral of light in her deepest place. When they get together they realise the One they have always been. They are One playing two. They know they are already in union, cannot ever be apart. They have always been One, non-dual.

The belief is that when man and woman see each other in attraction, their pull is about wanting and needing and all the sheaths and masks that they still want to keep intact. That is a mind game. The true light of attraction is that they are already One.

When you meet the Feminine Principle or the light of the Feminine in a woman, the Masculine Principle or the light of the Masculine in a man, you are not going to keep those sheaths for too long. You are even going to do battle to keep them in place between each other. The world is that battle. If you are true, those sheaths will come off fast so that you can realise that you have always been One and there has never been two. When you really meet in that place, a lot is going to move, reveal and be shed so that Knowing gets to see the game, gets to see it inside, outside and everywhere.

A lot of bowing down is needed in the meeting of the Masculine and the Feminine, in man and woman, in this world. You have to bow down. When you have bowed down enough, you come up changed - new consciousness, brighter, deeper, freer, more available for the movement of real life.

Death In Divine Loving

"Clean death is life lived to the full.
Full Awareness, full Consciousness,
full openness, full giving away, no holding back.

Clean death leads to clean life,
which leads to Self-enlightenment because
you are in the same way as your being,
nothing held onto - ALL GIVEN.

Not the way of this world,
but the way of your being."

21

The Original Tear

"To feel The Tear and not to run is to go through death and beyond."

Woman thinks she is separate from man, man thinks he is separate from woman, that they are two entities. They are the same one. They are the same heart.

When they became principles of the universe as the Masculine and the Feminine, they remained the same one in different displays of consciousness, movement, light and energy. When they arrive in a human body, woman believes that man is separate from her and man believes woman is separate from him. That is what I call 'The Tear'.

The whole point of this manifest universe is that man and woman are in the pull to realise they are one.

When woman denies that man is the other side of her heart and man denies that woman is the other side of his heart, they will feel The Tear where they made themselves into two. This is the deep inherent pain in humanity.

When man and woman are really called in the nature of God, The Tear comes home. When The Tear begins to come home, woman runs one way and man runs the other way. Sometimes woman doesn't run and wonders why he does. Other times man doesn't run, and wonders why she does.

The ones that don't' run and remain knowing The Tear, are the divine hope for life on earth.

To feel The Tear is to go through death and beyond. If a man and woman can feel The Tear and not run, all their past sexual activities will burn up in the nature of love.

They must feel The Tear. It has to be felt in the body all the way through. The Tear is the belief that they are two but they are one. In a man, this is in the nature of loving woman as his heart embodied. He will come to a terrible place of pain and if he stays there, he will realise that his pursuit of her was just a game because she is already one with him. If he stays present, his heart will explode and he will no longer need her. In that moment, he truly loves her, but he has to get to this place.

It happens in a similar way for a woman. If she stays present in The Tear with a man who is also ready to stay present in it, The Tear will heal and they begin to realise true love, true life and the purpose and meaning of attraction in existence. They enter into God.

Look around and you will see the avoidance of The Tear. It is everywhere. It creates the world. The world is the manifestation of our own manipulation of making man and woman two and not one. The world arises out of that disjointedness. The earth is waiting for union, bringing the two halves together. The earth is ready for a cosmic being of love to arrive, embodying true man and true woman.

You know The Tear in your body. Any pain whatsoever is The Tear whether it is a broken leg, cancer or a broken heart. Whatever pain there is, emotional or mental, is The Tear. When you feel and go through The Tear you are healing humanity as a being.

The Tear cannot touch who you are. Don't be frightened of it. Your self will become incredibly vulnerable and this is why most people turn away from The Tear. Jesus called it the 'eye of the needle'. Same thing. Go into The Tear and through it speak of the truth that you are knowing in the heart.

When your self belongs to your heart and deeper, you will find that your body can be, know and speak the truth of love. You are building a different kind of field through the calling of loving and knowing the goodness that God or truth is in the depths of your self. In being radically true, regardless of the cost of feeling The Tear, you begin to generate a new human experience for all beings on the planet to be free.

The Fear Of The Tear

*"A heart that is not afraid to be touched by pain is a heart
that will open into great love and great freedom."*

What we fear in our calling to unite our consciousness of the
Masculine, our consciousness of the Feminine, our bodies,
our life, and our bodies of Awareness, is feeling The Tear of
the heart that took place when One became two. We fear the
realisation of the tearing of the heart, the heart of God where
God tore God's heart into two, man and woman. The heart is
still one even though it is torn, but we avoid feeling The
Tear.

We avoid feeling it by believing that we are two, man is
'over here' and woman is 'over there'. We are intensely
attracted to putting the heart back together as one body, one
Consciousness, freedom itself. In the same instant, we realise
that The Tear in the heart, which is duality, is the process of
man and woman. It is the core process of duality, the belief
that we are two, that there is 'man and woman' and not God,
Pure Consciousness or pure life.

True Love's Claim - The Emptying Out

*"Dying for love, great lovers give up their present existence
and move into the higher spaces and places of knowing and
feeling beyond their separate sense of self, merging into their
higher calling of being together manifesting the forms of
their higher union."*

When we are called as man and woman in a true pull to the
reality of oneness, this empties both man and woman in body
and mind. The emptying out shows us what we, as
Consciousness, have put into our heart about our egoic self
and our disconnection with the universe, with love and with
another.

The moment we truly step into relating as love in deep
sexual intimacy that immediately starts the divine work of
emptying out every level of the body-mind instrument to be
filled up with the connection and the communion of love
that we are called to bring here. This new love is never about
a self. It is about our being.

Real intimate connection is when the beingness of the
Masculine and the beingness of the Feminine truly meet and
truly merge. That is when we know love. This is because the
true state of the earth is that there is only one Being that
seems to be split into two frequencies or principles - the
Masculine and the Feminine, embodied as man and woman.
We look at each other as separate. Woman believes man is
separate from her and man looks at woman as separate from

him, yet we have this loud, loud calling appearing in our attraction to man and woman, particularly when we love God or truth or love. We have this knowing that there is so much more to a man, so much more to a woman than just 'man and woman' as selves. It is divinity that calls us together for us to realise that we have always been one.

We are two frequencies in the one power of universal energy of love and profundity. We are already that One. When we are drawn together, we begin to empty out all the pain, the disconnection, the wrong knowledge, the misuse of sexual power and the distorted use of our sexuality. All of this begins to empty out.

It simply means we didn't know any better. We were never taught the divine secrets. True lovers need the knowledge of the process of divine loving otherwise we begin to fight each other. We can see that fight, the belief that man and woman are two, in the world.

Anywhere there is a fight whether it is a war in the world or in the cells of the body or in a heated conversation on the street, it is the fight between man and woman in their distorted knowledge, their belief that they are separate. This fight purposely keeps us apart because somewhere we know that the calling to be One involves the healing of the belief that we were ever two. This is why we are called to make love. Somewhere we know we have something to gift each other, to re-unite each other into the oneness of our true soul, our true intimacy.

To step into such an intimate relationship, we need to understand that this kind of loving initiates emptying, not only of your past as a man or woman, but your father's past, your mother's past, your cultural past. You begin to see, "My God! The battle I have been experiencing with man, with woman, is on the whole planet as separation. The pain that I feel is not just my personal pain, it is the pain of separation between every human being and it is all focused in The Tear between my self and this new man, this new woman, in my life."

We are that that heals the universe of man and woman or that that tears the universe of man and woman apart. The healing of this world is up to how man and woman love God or truth, their True Self, together.

There is beautiful truth in meeting the subconscious. When love truly is, love reclaims every aspect of the cosmos, every aspect of man and of woman. Love reclaims the spaces of distortion and realigns them with the true purpose of love's calling, which is union. Every place within the sphere of man and woman is awakened to the light that is calling and this very light reveals the patterns of your old sexuality, your control, your fears and your doubts.

This is the death that man and woman *must* walk in, but walk in as their Pure Being, as their real calling to love. This is where the healing is, where the self-mastery is and the re-alignment of man and woman into oneness. Every aspect of man and woman is awoken and that then moves into the world.

You can see that Masculine and Feminine power asleep is manipulating and controlling our societies, our culture, the world. Masculine and feminine power awakened in the heart is not controlling. It is creating for all beings to be free, for all beings to know their own true heart's love and divinity, their own possibility to create a new universe. All this comes about in man and woman who are truly moved towards the highest intimacy.

It is a total reorientation of life. That means man and woman are going to have to be two brave souls belonging to a greater truth than they are currently moving in the selves. They have to learn to move only in the deeper places within their heart and within each other's heart, knowing that this will bring storms of emptying out. Our capacity to belong to the truth deep within our being, deep within our heart is our growing capacity to create love in the likeness of our divine Self.

This is when the real Masculine and real Feminine beingness presents itself to the other and one can have experiences of the presentation of the Masculine to the Feminine or the Feminine to the Masculine. One can experience higher domains of intimacy, truly divine, but one has to let go of everything that is arising as a problem and begin to see that difficulties are doorways to an entirely new orientation of love's guidance to purify one's own body-mind, one's own self and the self of this world.

The love between man and woman has never been about anything else but the transformation of the earth and the universe. That is how big our love is. Somewhere we know this. That is why we are so inspired to love each other but it seems to go haywire because we don't go the whole way. We are thrown off course by our likes and dislikes instead of staying with what we know to be true. An ongoing mutual encouragement and a true attraction is needed.

Until we deepen enough in the knowing of who we really are, we must be clear that we call a partner that is on the same wavelength or at least starting to walk that wavelength. As you start to walk and call for a deeper intimacy of love, your self is still going to be calling all the pretenders. Somewhere amongst all the pretenders there is real potential. It is up to the depth of you being in your heart to call that forth but you have to walk and live it together. You must become bonded in your being for that journey to be taken.

In divine love, we face all the places where we haven't been all that we can be with another. We face the vulnerability of our hearts and of the self-defenses we put around and into our heart. We face all the instruments of deception that we have put into our self since childhood. We become very vulnerable as we move towards a greater divine love and a deeper connectivity in our making of love. We begin to discover in the real making of love, that the making of love is not for our self, it is for our being. We begin to make love as beings and that purifies our cells. We begin to be men and women that are personified in the love that we are being and becoming.

In all the things we face, that maybe our parents, brothers and sisters couldn't resolve, we are being called from the very bottom of our heart, from the very ancient place of our Masculine and Feminine power. We are called to really be true with this and to love enough to take this journey of transforming man and woman into oneness in our lives.

The journey most definitely means you will be facing your self. Man and woman are artists at bringing up each other's self. When we know what is really taking place, it becomes an entirely different dance, one where incredible healing can take place and we leap into new places together. We grow so much more as men and women loving the divine, loving being true, loving being together. We grow so much quicker in that kind of union.

24

The Undoing Of The World

*"Awake! Awake man and woman and realise you are one.
You unfold each other's destiny as that One
and it manifests as the manner in which we live on this
planet either as universal beings or as fools."*

When you first see each other and there is a real connection
and you are willing to go towards that connection no matter
what the cost to your self or your life, the wonderment of the
mystery you are moving in undoes the limited sense of self
of woman and she begins to shine. It undoes the limited
sense of self and consciousness of man and he starts to know
deeply and shine.

In that, they walk through hell together and this hell appears
in the world. We are seeing it right now as war and conflict.
We are also seeing their love - birds are singing, flowers are
flowering, nature is wild, oceans are moving, stars are
shining. Everything is happening because of their oneness
love.

To reach this in a realised innermost place together, to know
that union is already here and manifest, is the undoing of
how you relate and how you direct what you believe is your
life. This life is already what you are and is already moving
in a profound direction.

25

Dancing On Your Own Grave

"Death is the complete and absolute surrender to what is real in our depth. The only thing that dies is past which gets lifted up and integrated into this vast, vast space of Now, because in reality nothing dies."

Real tantra has profound direction, that's the Masculine, He has profound meaning and purpose. Real tantra has real value, that's the Feminine in how She dances, displays Herself and gives form to Her great love.

He, the direction of life, claims Her, the energy, abundance, light and fragrance that dances into form the one direction of all life. This is a hell of a dance!

One who truly lives tantra is one whose actions are a response to that that created this, one whose actions are an absolute, deep response to Source.

Our invitation as individuals is to be deep. Our invitation is to constantly reach deeper. This means a breaking, a shattering of the shallow. Depth does this, depth shatters the shallow.

I am talking about a profound love, where our whole field is open for whatever experience comes. No defenses. All there will be is a profound surrender of what came before, an utter dropping away of what was and a dropping through into more of what really is. This is what starts to come alive in such a one. Such a one is endlessly deep.

Real tantra is dancing on your own grave, constantly. It is a love of death in an utter 'Yes!' to life.

Deep Sexuality Embodied

*"When your sexuality is really coming forth from your heart,
you are enabled to read the mystery of the earth
and the universe and the mystery of another that you may
have the calling to know love with.*

*That is a transmission of beingness that has all your forms,
all your body and all your life, so you are able to move
deeply into this life and into your union with God in another,
with the divine in another, through You.*

*You are knowing with your being what sexuality really is.
It is singing in the birds, it is moving in the skies, it is in all
creatures and in all things and it is light that marries it and
moves it. It is a movement of love."*

26

The Most Sacred Event On The Planet

"The manifest movement of the universe is a movement of pure sexual energy. It is the means by which beingness moves, communes and communicates what it is into form."

Sexuality is completely sacred. It is the most sacred event on the planet or anywhere in the universe. Everything you can see in this universe of form has come about through the true sexuality of the total union of the two principles of the manifest universe, the Masculine and Feminine, Shiva and Shakti or Yin and Yang, for they have never been apart. They are ceaselessly making love and are in union. They are completely and utterly one, yet they remain absolutely and completely two, two principles as one love.

The energy of sexuality is a primal energy through which Source moves. It moves sexual energy through and into the bodies. When Source or your being engages sexuality, there is a sacred entrance into the innermost place of wonder and beauty. When held to be sacred and embodied in the heart, sexuality opens the universal mind of man, the universal womb of woman and the universal heart of all beings.

In pure sexuality, we are learning how to hold the space of that sacred energy, not to use it from the conditional patterns of mind, emotion, neediness or cultural and religious structures that are forcibly endeavouring to control us and keep us separate and fearful.

Sexuality is a primal energy field that the entire cosmos is moving from. Beyond sexuality is the pure beingness that sexuality comes from. Being is the One making love and not a 'someone' making love.

Sexuality remains undistorted when we as men and women come home to our being. Sexuality in the hands of our mind and in the arms of our emotion is pain, confusion and all manner of distortion. When we engage in sexuality for a 'me', we settle for less than love and a mental emotional body that cannot deliver what love really is, cannot deliver eternity, cannot deliver a profound opening into reality which a man and a woman who truly love God can.

A man can only love fearlessly if he does not love for himself. A woman can only open fearlessly if what she opens to is not for her self. That kind of loving opens to the immeasurable. During that loving, reality opens up within and flows. Suddenly there is even greater love and purpose and finer creativity because man and woman are vessels of another place entirely.

Her love heals the wound of seeming birth. His love heals the wound of supposed death. If there is no divine connection to that other place through self-sacrifice or self-knowing, that place does not open and nourish the loving. Then we invent all manner of things to fill the gap.

The only thing that can ever fulfil a man or woman is not a man or woman, but the source that man and woman come from. Higher woman is a woman who begins to give herself back to her being. As she gives herself back to her being, she belongs to no man, she is one with God. When a man who has also given himself back to God, who is not belonging to a woman, meets with her, they are in the love of One God Consciousness. They are really together. That is a marriage made in heaven. That is what is taking place. Their love is not just everlasting, it is eternal. They have united the very principles in a living way whilst they have bodies and they will never be apart.

A man or woman coming to you is the 'experiential field' but the coupling and union of the consciousness is not experiential. That is real love. True man and woman are making this daring leap to a place that morality or the world cannot hold them back from. They now belong to eternity. They do not belong to the world. They are a super God-conscious man and woman, a new man and woman. There will be no world, there will be the earth.

We do know there is God on this earth in sacred sexuality. We know also how we use and abuse sexuality to get a level of comfort because we will not face the self that we have come to transform. The whole point in the real love of the Feminine and Masculine is to love God or truth together, which means: 'What is the truth of the moment?' That truth reveals: 'I know this is a pattern displaying itself.' In that knowing, the beauty and deliciousness, the silence and the wonderful raging passion that can take place between two people that profoundly love, opens you to real knowledge. It opens you to truth. It opens you to what love really is.

There is a yearning in the conscious humanness of a human being to unite, the yearning of God to know God, the union of the Beloved to know the Beloved, the interface of the two aspects of the Pure Consciousness and form to come together. That is the yearning of the Masculine and Feminine, which comes down as man and woman. It is the yearning of the whole cosmos to know its source, to unify and fully embody what it is.

Sexuality must be returned to the heart, must be returned to truth, not some conceptual truth, but the truth of one's own being. It transcends all.

True sexuality has no need of morality because when embodied in truth, it is beyond all the vehicles of perception. No moral code is needed because wholeness is the direct experience. If one is truly centred in the heart of pure Knowing, it becomes beautifully and wonderfully clear.

There is a knowing: 'This is pure.' There is no movement of mind, no movement of feeling other than when love comes through the mind, comes through feeling. You are in a true sacred movement of opening, opening to the place where sexuality comes from, the pure place of your being. You are able as consciousness of woman, as consciousness of man, to see from a pure mind, to feel from a pure heart and a pure womb space. You are able to enter the sacred dimensions of the continual flowering of higher and higher love.

27

Love Undoes Borrowed Light

"To know you are infinite Consciousness, you play the game of falling out of it and become finite. A finite moment is a small slice of your infinite experience. Through you falling out of your infinite Self and becoming finite, you have the possibility of stabilising in the mystery of the Real You."

Our sexuality is moved by the heart, by beingness, the moment 'I Am Here', instantly. When I say 'I', I am not speaking of a particular person. I point to the only 'I' in the universe, which is at the core of every person. The moment 'I Am Here', Awareness, beingness and pure sexuality are manifesting the universe that I experience as real Consciousness, its movement and its forms of expression.

You seem to get lost when you land in a self that bears no resemblance to your original nature and yet that is the game we are playing, endlessly - the game of return home, return to express, return home, return to express, return home. You play this game until you realise that your likes and dislikes, your fears and desires hold you prisoner in the form you believe you are as a body-mind, as a particular man or a woman, as the self you are given.

In truth, the limited sense of self arrives when You, Awareness, come. You as Awareness land in a limited self that is inherited. You inherited a part of this universe although you actually pervade it as Consciousness. You inherit sexuality although sexuality moves the stars into form. You inherited this body to discover what you are because without it you are in the unseen. With it, you can see. Whilst you have form you can see and know You as Awareness, knowing itself.

As man and woman, when your sexuality moves one with your being, this is a movement of love. When it moves from identification with your self or person, it will display a split, a split between the Principles of the Masculine and Feminine, a split between man and woman.

You have arrived here in a level of self but who you are is not limited or even obscured. You just have to turn to where you are knowing You, Awareness, being man, being woman, being human. Turn your Awareness to the light of your knowing. Stop borrowing light from the moon. The moon is borrowed light. It is reflecting the light or the energy of the sun. Thoughts and feelings of your past, yours or anyone else's, are all borrowed light or information.

Borrowed light or information does not return you to realise who and what you are. Borrowed light does not move your sexuality into pure openness of immediate forms of the love you are, which opens the door to what you are within. With borrowed light, you try to move and control your life, your person, your self, your sexuality, your lover, your this and your that. You ceaselessly project borrowed information onto others but in truth, you are only ever reading your self. You are either reading the light that you first are, the light you came in with that still seats itself silently at your heart, or the borrowed light you created your self with.

You cannot avoid sexuality whilst you have a body. Your body is made out of sexuality. In the deepest or highest place, your sexuality is pure, one with the universe. It is of the same stuff that makes the universe. It is Pure Consciousness, one half unseen, one half seen. There is more in the unseen than there is in the seen. The seen is 'borrowed light', the forms of your separate sense of self. The unseen is what you are.

When You as Awareness look from the deep into the forms of existence, sexuality moves to form the experience of Consciousness moving to a deeper place of Being. That deeper place of Being comes into manifestation, not just for manifestation, but so that what you are as the Consciousness that is moving and creating this man, this woman, can know a deeper place of meaning.

You believe your sexuality is in your root chakra and not your entire body and life, but in truth, all the forms you identify with are your sexuality. If you still believe you are a particular man or a particular woman, then those forms are unintegrated forms of your being.

As a man, if your calling is to know love or God though woman, woman will show you your unintegrated forms. In her mystery, she will point to unseen places within you, unmet in your body and in your consciousness. She doesn't know that she's doing this but that's what happens if you choose to listen to your first light, your knowing, and not to the borrowed light, the forms of your separate sense of self.

Everything you have is sexuality moving. What do you move it with? Do you move it as a self? Do you move it as a person? Do you move it belonging to the world? Does your self belong to the world? Does your self belong to your separate sensed self or to your heart? Have you returned everything, every form of you, into your heart?

In a true calling, she comes to you to come completely into your heart and you return all the forms you are knowing her with within you, back to your heart. No small thing to bring about in a lifetime.

When your sexuality is given to the truth of You, you will experience deep awakening and much experience of death on the level of your self and person. You will see levels of you that project and have set mechanisms in place to keep your body-mind identity unchanged. In this way, you won't call to you a deeper participation in your own awakening and a change of the cells of this very earth. You won't call this to you because it will change you so much, you won't be able to live and move from borrowed light anymore.

If the truth of You has deeper meaning for you than how you have been identifying yourself through your sexuality, then you are in a deep awakening possibility. You will go through many deaths as everything that you believe describes you, inside and out, undoes.

Even in all the little things, you will see how all this works, how when you get home you do what your self wants even though you are knowing a deeper level that calls for so much more. Your self wants to sit down. Your self wants to rest. Your self wants to watch the TV. Your self just wants to do things for itself. But what do the deeper levels of you call for?

Listen to the deeper levels of you and respond. That raises not only your consciousness but your sexuality. Deeper levels of your body open, deeper levels of your being open. You will enjoy a beingness that is instantly fulfilled on every level. Habits just dissolve because they carry no energy for you anymore. You are no longer interested in borrowed light. True meaning opens up and begins to move.

28

In Ancient Cultures We Were Initiated Into Sexuality

"What we are truly here for is divine love, not as a concept but as a direct experience."

In ancient cultures, we were initiated into our sexuality by elders who had a degree of integrated consciousness and experience on higher levels. They were touching upon the spiritual essence of One Self and the universe in their relationship and had enough integrated consciousness to say to the children of the tribe: "This is my genuine learned experience of the universe, untainted by personal experience. I offer you this knowledge." Initiation rites for young men and young women coming into puberty were an essential part of life.

We can widely see the distortions that arise from not being given the rite of entry into our sexuality from the deepest place of our real being. Most of us have not been initiated into pure sexuality, honorability and the sacredness of being together in that union, so we confuse the sexual act with personal considerations rather than personal transcendence. We pass this on from generation to generation and create a society based on likes and dislikes, 'haves and have–nots', goal orientation aimed at survival. We wreck the planet, wreck our sexuality and begin to cover up our real heart's longing for the realisation of our divine light to live in our embodiment. We become materialists.

What we are truly here for is divine love not as a concept but as a direct experience. Man, your call to the Feminine is clear and real and nourishing, but you have to be drawn to Her from your real inner experience and to bring greater consciousness into your self and person on all levels. In that way, instead of going to a woman unconsciously, you are realising those levels that are drawn to her for your self. When I say your 'self', what self is, is beautiful, what self is, is a canvas full of paint. Human beings have this terrible idea about self. All it needs is self-mastery of the one and only Self, hidden in the secret place of your divine heart nature. It needs to be recognised in you, then your self is not a problem but a gift, a gift bestowed on Thee by the blessed One, who you are in the deep. You must bless your self. You bless it by being radically real and caring of it from ever deeper, higher places of love and realised knowledge. Speak to it: "This is the way, self." In that way, you shape it.

The Feminine is the healing of body, mind and emotion that can go right to a man's soul. The Masculine is the healing of the body, mind and her creativity and expression. He can be ever growing deeper presence and that is very healing for woman and for this earth.

The Masculine is a vertical reality. Masculine Consciousness is vertical. In that verticality, life moves and evolves. It has no past as a pattern or programming that has future. It is vertical, always Here, present Now, the one and only reality this very instant. There is no past and yet it is filled with pure potential, which could be called its future. It will never ever have existed before, for it only exists Now.

When a woman sees the light of the Masculine, her lower self that is not integrated with the profound openness and love that she is, mistakes man for the Masculine that she is experiencing. She mixes up lower levels of attraction that originate in personal likes and dislikes because she has not learned to open fully and allow all things to just be in her openness no matter what it looks like. She has not realised the radiance of love. She has made a concept of it.

Woman, when you are truly touched by man and it is real, you are touched by the Pure Consciousness of the Masculine. It is not the man. If there is a real calling and it touches you deeply, that pull is to the Masculine Principle beyond the man. It is not necessarily beyond his experience. This is dependent on whether the consciousness of the Masculine has been lived in the man's experience, if he has integrated depth of consciousness. He may have opened to the profound Masculine depth, which is endless in existence and never ceases to deepen. It doesn't suddenly stop. It is evolutionary otherwise God would be finite, a 'known'. God can never be known, because God is Now.

The discovery of what the Masculine light is in a man and the Feminine light is in a woman is like peeling back layers of an onion. You are stripped naked. Everything comes flying off including everything that you didn't want to have coming off. Each layer contains a layer of experience that you have deadened and not come alive to. All that that gets stripped off and within each moment of stripping off is the realisation of the profound light of Real Self contained within each layer. In truth, there is nothing but Real Self masquerading as patterns of egoity. Nonetheless, the stripping back and the seeing of egoity, allowing it to come in fully embodied in your experience, is the discovery that within every painful pattern is the light yet to be known as you.

If man and woman are called together, they have to know this otherwise their life is going to be hell. Most men and women stop that process and seek to create a safe and secure plastic world of comfort, which is the cause of all human suffering from wars to disease to famine. It is a world that could well lead to the destruction of most of humanity. Those that remain would discover what has always been here on a profound level of Being - the nakedness of the earth spirit totally connected with the cosmos. Divinity is instantly known because there is no egoity around to distort it.

Man and woman represent far more than a body-mind having relationships that sometimes work and sometimes don't. They are a link to a vast spiritual field that connects the earth with numerous suns and their planets, forming a cosmic matrix of evolving consciousness. Together, the Masculine and Feminine inform the earth, through man and woman, of the possibility of universal potential manifesting on earth.

29

Sexuality Beyond The Root Chakra

"Lighten up around your sexuality!
Let it go from your root chakra.
Know it as the light of your heart and its movement, the very
impulse that moves formlessness into form.

If we were to mention the word 'sex' anywhere at all, be it on the street, in a supermarket or at work, people immediately bring their attention and energy to their genital area or root chakra as if that is what sex is about but it really isn't. That is just one very small area of where sexual energy rests or belongs or explores the universe.

Sexual energy is to have *all* the levels of the body. It is very much the same as the universe we all exist in. The entire universe is sexual energy moving and moving with integrated consciousness. This is what produces the stars and the planets, it is what creates life and what evolves both life and Consciousness.

As long as we keep sex as something happening just in the genital area and we don't allow it to have our heart, our sexuality becomes something we use to control life and circumstances with. It becomes something we use for our self to become and to maintain a particular type of man and a particular type of woman.

When sex is given to the whole body, to every level of the body all the way through and we bring our body in alignment with the universe, sexuality becomes a fineness of attunement to the entire body of the cosmos. It is no longer a limited experience of 'just sex' or 'having sex' but entirely holy and abundant in its nature of loving. It becomes subtle and pure and begins to be the means through which we know and communicate with a flower, a bird or a star, through which we know and commune with another's heart.

In truth, sexuality is the sacred instrument in which Pure Consciousness and pure form realise their union. It is a divine instrument that communicates evolution and transmits the more of what we are in the deep.

Sexuality is not just contained in the genitals or the root chakra. It is supposed to arise throughout the whole body entirely belonging to the heart. In this, control is given up by the forces of sexual power and is returned to the power of the heart. Only when our sexuality is returned to the power of the heart do we become fully rested, fully available and fully alive in the uniqueness of our own divinity. Now we are truly able to explore that divinity with others in the universe of our relationships. Now we enter an intimacy that is purely divine and able to enter both deeper levels of consciousness and of the body.

The body isn't just this physical figure. The body is endlessly deeper than what you know in sense perception, so when our sexuality is returned to our heart and allowed to have the whole of our body, we become the pure intimacy of love that is spontaneously creating the universe.

Sexuality belongs to the pure heart. It belongs to that that has no past. When sexuality moves from a power of love that has no past, it creates true relationship and true forms. Our bodies are purified by the intimate movement of sexuality belonging to the heart. There is the undoing of old patterns, which is part and parcel of the death cycle to enter into new life. When sexuality returns to the heart, there is spontaneous innermost connection with love, our own love, with our lover and the people with whom we commune and communicate.

Sex then is no longer about a genital area where everyone is psychically running around to get something out of sexuality. It is deeply pure and it becomes a divine movement where we know each other beyond our body-mind and in our body-mind on deeper levels. It is a very healing place, one that heals, recreates and realigns one's sexuality and one's purpose to exist with one's own divine contract to be the light of love in the universe and in our relationships. It is the purifier for everything that we know is truly good.

30

Shaped By Love Or Sex

"In how you connect with your sexual field, you are learning that you can connect through your sexuality with the entire universe."

Sexuality is not just about the root chakra. It is about the root of how the universe moves and forms the union of Pure Consciousness and pure sexual energy. It is the profound that spills out of the Self and forms the experience of the universe.

Sex not freed from your subconscious will move your life in distortion away from your real heart and knowing. You will make dualities or opposites of having a body, knowing woman, knowing man, knowing the sexual field and the nature of consciousness. You will be moving in assumptions and conclusions through experience that was not enlivened by what you truly belong to at the core of your heart.

Your self is actually shaped by whether you make love or have sex. Making love is the union of Awareness-Knowing moving as the body expressed. That is pure radiant sexuality. Sex is just sex, moving for the experience of a self that is formed and conditioned only by wants and needs, a self that doesn't actually exist. It affects how you move and live your life. Making love doesn't affect your life. It *is* your life.

31

The Making Of Love Gives Entrance Into The Heart

"The real making of love is a way of lovemaking that turns your self into what love is."

The moment we say 'sexuality', we always think of the root chakra. That is not the truth. The stars are made of sexuality, the planets are sexuality, everything is sexual energy moved by the pure light of Being. That is your original nature. As Awareness, as a being, every movement of you is sexuality.

When you make a choice to move and do something, the moving and doing is the moving and doing of your sexual energy. Pure sexuality moves by your being when you as Awareness respond completely to your heart. It is spontaneous and utterly pure. When it moves with your man, with your woman and it moves from light, that is the making of love.

The making of love gives you entrance into each other. Sex doesn't. It keeps you on the surface and disturbs every level of you. The making of love gives you entrance into each other's heart as one and the same being. It gives you entrance into levels of your body that are unseen and mystical levels of your body open by you being pure in your response to each other. Now your sexuality moves by the deeper beingness of both of you.

As a woman, when a man reaches you in a pure moment of seeing you, he can move to levels of your body that you don't even know you have. This is why you feel such love and union with him. If he does not use any level of past to move his mind, move his self, his person to move towards you then he has deeper access to what you are than you do. This opens deeper levels of his consciousness that are deeper than the levels that reached you. It is like a figure eight. It is a transmission of endless light and a pure movement of the sacredness of what you really are.

Within that, there will be the undoing of the levels of your self and your person and you will experience them coming up through your body, your mind, through your old sexuality. You will need to love so much that you both master the self in moving together in a deeper meaning than you ever moved with any man or woman in your life.

Sexuality then is power, the awesome power of the Feminine Principle that gives instant form to what Consciousness is. You have landed in a level of expression for you to raise this level up and open even deeper. This is the real calling of man and woman together, not to keep each other the same but to enter each other deeper than ever before and heal the past with real light, real love, real union, all at the level of the heart and deeper. This purifies your heart, your sexuality and your forms.

32

Sex Just Isn't 'It'

"True sexuality is being openness. It is the complete and utter letting go of all ideas of who you are."

Man and woman play a sexual game with each other when they keep their sexuality in attraction instead of moving in a true calling to unite as that that has no opposite. They can have as much sex as they want but it will not change them. Only when their sexual energy is given to their heart fully, do they begin to commune as a being throughout every cell of the universe and as their body. They begin to move as love itself. Sex means nothing anymore. It is entirely returned to their heart so when they make love, the calling actually demonstrates itself in them. It is alive and real and of the highest value. It is the only marriage they truly want, the marriage of being real. Nothing else outside fulfills them.

When man and woman really come together in union, sex just isn't 'it' anymore. The need to get excitement is shallow and coarse. They still see it in the world and occasionally even in their selves but they now recognise what it is and begin to know the movement of love in the sexual realm of their selves. They realise that sexual energy is the fullness of their being and this fullness cannot be activated unless it springs from and belongs to their heart. Everything changes in their life. It is not that they have less fear or struggle but they know the struggle is in their separate sense of self and they are bringing that into union.

33

Always Know Deeper Than What You Are Knowing Now

"Man and woman are a profound process of awakening and self-transformation. Leap into the process to know the love that is possible. Allow the process to move through you and awaken to the 'No-process love."

If you have used your sexuality for your self, this is what you are afraid of. You are afraid that man will undo this in you, and he will. He actually wants to know your heart. In knowing your heart, your sexual energy is a blessing that makes him come into his body and he begins to know true embodiment.

A man who has never loved a woman is not in his body. He is still in his head and he finds it difficult to love woman with full abandonment of his self. When he really loves her utterly, regardless of the shadows that come out of him or her, his being drops fully into his body. When a man embodies his being, he is able to fill all that you are regardless of what you do. He knows where you are moving and how you are, even before you do.

If you are a woman awakening to really know the union in your heart and in a partnership, you love that he knows this and that he is not running from it. You love it. He is able to allow you to see and know him thoroughly, for your consciousness and your energy to fully enter him. He has the joy of fully coming into your heart, your body, and something new comes out of that, new for both of you. It begins to have earth, water, fire, air and ether and it comes Here. All the elements turn into a triangle or trinity where man and woman are one moving beingness. Everything begins to look and feel different.

There are moments in this kind of love when everything is so transparent, that you both experience liquid movement. A liquid movement where you are moving on greater levels of beingness as One than you ever thought possible.

Always know deeper than what you are knowing now. Know deeper, cease separating the elements from who you are and from your beingness.

In the union of the Masculine and the Feminine, you then begin to realise an electromagnetic field that begins to build a whole new life. Man and woman do not know that they produce an electromagnetic field. It is vast. You have the power to manifest new forms of real love.

Whilst you keep him away and her away, not fully met, all that you manifest is more of the same thing and keep your selves separate. When he draws you fully into your heart and fully into your body and you draw him fully into his consciousness and fully into his heart and body, a whole new sphere of life begins to be yours.

Whilst all this is coming about, you will face more of the process of man and woman than you ever did before, it speeds up. There is much work to be done – your self to be emptied, new form to be made, old form to dissolve. This is all very natural.

In refusing the process of man and woman, you hold the old patterns together and they gain momentum. You actually make yourself more separate. Go into the process of man and woman without endeavouring to make everything better. You are well trained to seek false comfort over what is true. You choose to live a pretty life together and not the dynamic dance of love that makes everything new as the old disappears.

In your life, you will see that you mostly reference through past, really old past. You relate through past wanting and needing, through likes and dislikes, mainly in order to avoid a repeat of what you believe created your past. In truth, you created your past by not being the presence of Knowing, the truth in your heart.

When you let this go, you are no longer about being old together. You are about being new together and the new together isn't you as selves. The new together is the recognition of what you are entering into, that you are moving in another place. This place Here makes it possible for the depth of your divine beingness to have form. You get to awaken to and know Here, what you cannot know when you are in that place because there is no one to know it. Only Here can you know what you are and it can have form.

Whilst you maintain old forms in this life, you die with old forms. You remain stuck with old form, it leaves you for a while until you are drawn again into a body.

While you are making new form, not for your self, but as a natural response to what you know is true, new form simply happens. You begin to experience new form. It is so subtle, so real in your heart, so gentle and fulfilling that you begin to be filled up.

You must go all the way into the process of man and woman, all the places that your father's father, mother's mother did not move on. Only the process brings you out new. You awaken to who you are as the Principle of the Feminine, as the Principle of the Masculine, the One.

Conversations

"Woman's form and man's form are the creative movement necessary for attraction to evolve into a calling. Whilst attraction is sex wanting and needing, pure sexuality is the manifestation of love and its greater calling.

The essence of woman is a movement and manifestation of truth, not woman but truth, manifesting as love's potential as woman, embodied only Now.

When man responds as truth to the essence of woman as love, pure sexuality moves full of the heart of Being.

The only question is: Will man and woman die to self and all its forms to manifest love? This is definitely the most uncomfortable time man and woman will ever experience as they undo whilst recreating themselves as the movement and forming of love."

34

When You're Tired of Sex, Lovemaking Begins

Interview with Robert Lubarski - Denmark

"You cannot separate the bedroom from what you do, how you do it and why you do it, from walking down the street to buying your groceries to meeting people."

Q: B, when I look at the world I see this urge everywhere. It is almost desperate, like we want to find the ignition for sex all the time. It's in the magazines, it's everywhere, as if we are afraid of losing our 'horny-ness' and yet there is this longing to know deeper.

Then there are all those ideas that monogamous relationships don't work. People are leaving each other, have sex with other partners without saying, lying to each other etc. Many people are single and in that they talk about polyamory but I have a feeling that there is a deeper possibility in our intimacy and it is opening right now for us as human beings.

B: I would add more to much of what you said, and I would put it slightly differently. I wouldn't say that monogamous relationships don't work. I would say what doesn't work is not being aligned with your heart in any relationship.

That leaves you totally open for your heart to move where you relate from and to what you relate. Your heart alone chooses how you move in this life and not you as the belief that you are a separate entity, a self or an ego identity.

What one is, is a profundity that is behind everyone, regardless of how their self has been constructed. It is deep meaning and to connect with that deeper meaning, one has to awaken from the belief of being a separate sense of self. That happens mysteriously. When you are ripe something opens in you in that you know more than your experience and more than your sexual experience.

Q: Explain 'ripe'.

B: Ripe means that for no particular reason your beingness has touched you deeper than your self-experience and you have known the touch or the calling of your being. Suddenly, in an instant, there is more meaning that does not get reflected by how you live. You are knowing more than your experience.

I would suggest that in anyone who is having sex, who is exploring sexuality, the deepest calling is to discover what sexuality really is, where it comes from and what the meaning behind it is. When you first move towards sexuality and explore it not from want and need but the communion and connection that you know you must go towards, somewhere in you, in that connection with another, you are developing an awakening and a power in which the universe moves. You are awakening to a deeper meaning of what you are and a deeper power of movement that is more than you as a separate sense of self, a movement that is moved by your heart.

When you move towards sexuality from want and need, sex becomes a power that distorts reality and you believe you are a 'someone' who needs something from another. You then experience sex for a 'me' that doesn't actually exist.

Everyone goes through this until they either awaken from that or not. If you are seriously discovering the love within yourself and the love within another, then you awaken from the need to have sex to the calling to discover true sexuality and the making of love. You might discover that true sexuality is a way in which you communicate and commune with the universe with your body and not just with your spirit or your being. This is the union of your being in your heart with your body. It is actually how you came into existence, the movement of your being and the movement of energy joined making the body. It is a lovemaking process that is eternal and that births stars. There is a deeper meaning behind sexuality and a power that doesn't belong to a particular someone but if you move into it as a 'sexual someone', that power becomes a tremendous distorted power that can move and manipulate your life and self.

If you awaken to what your sexuality really belongs to as a heart, you begin to have the ability to commune the mystery of what you are into the mystery of what another is. That opens up to the sublime movement of the meaning of why you would ever make love, be sexually alive from the heart with another. You are exploring the meaning behind what calls you to unite your bodies through your heart, through your mind, through your experience. There is something 'being made'. You become a porthole for what is beyond and the making of love brings it here. You begin to know it and it transforms your body, your mind, your sexuality, your life.

Q: That's very painful I find.

B: Painful only in that it exposes the use of self as a particular perceived someone who needs and wants something. The pain is only that the true making of love empties out the lower levels of the nervous system that were being used to have something for your self.

Q: I have times when I think sexuality is so noisy that I can't stand it. This whole story about sexuality that is in me… I can't stand it!

B: Well, you'll have to go through that. That's the level of self-development. If you are called to another through intimate union as Being and through having bodies, then your body and your nervous system will empty out how you used to move, how you used to pattern your sexuality. Your sexuality has a direct effect on how you are putting your life together, how you think, how you feel, what you do, how you do it, who for and what for. Sexuality is directly aligned with the movement of life and the universe. It is directly aligned with the movement of life as You. If your life belongs to a deeper meaning that you are endeavouring to point towards, a deeper meaning begins to open and you get to know the levels of your old self that you didn't know.

There needs to be forgiveness here and knowledge because a level of your old self will come up to be emptied. That is the pain you are speaking of. If you judge that level, you are still misinterpreting what this life is really about. You have to wake up from those lower levels of your sexuality, your body. Sexuality is the movement of the entirety of your life, not just your genital area. Sexuality then begins to be very clear how you know and feel the universe through a deeper enlightenment of heart-fullness. You are awakening.

Everything starts to come towards you in how you make love for the making of love and the understanding of what you are and who the other is. You are deepening into each other to know each other deeply. You will come upon realms of Pure Being and pure love that were impossible while you were having sex. Your being won't open to having sex, the mystery won't open to having sex, only pain and frustration will open with that. There will be an emptying of that as you re-orientate your sexuality, your life and your sexuality as an intimacy with another. As it re-orientates to moving from knowing in the heart, there will be self-emptying and also Self-enlightenment. You begin to know the presence of love. It won't be noisy. It will be still and deep. There will be more depth and a deeper sense of passion for life.

Pure Sexuality Includes Your Life In All Things

Q: I believe there are many, many couples out there who are really longing for this deepening with each other. Do you have any advice for this work?

B: First, higher sexuality or pure sexuality coupled with your love for another must include your life in all things. You cannot separate the bedroom from what you do, how you do it and why you do it, from walking down the street, to buying your groceries to meeting people.

You are learning to open your body and open your heart to all of life and respond to all of life. You are meeting it, fully in the body, fully in the heart regardless of how the self reacts. In that manner, you will find that your lovemaking is much deeper and sincere. You will be able to meet any rising pattern in each other, not as a problem, but from a discovery of what that patterns represents as it comes home to your deeper loving and your deeper communion with each other.

It is really believing that your love together, your sexuality together, is more than just having sex. It is discovering the mystery of being love - two beings loving, two beings discovering, two beings moving as one body, the mystery of each other. You then discover the mystery of life. As that really happens, it frees you up from the belief that your sexuality is just something in the bedroom. Your sexuality is what moves all of life and how you experience life.

As you free up your sexuality from just being in the bedroom you experience the abundance of a wonderful beautiful life and you know it everywhere. Through that, compassion develops and opens for how life moves and how it moves in different ways for many beings.

My guidance is more of an arrow of wisdom. Always be true to the level of your heart, with your self and with each other. Don't move away from what your heart knows regardless of how it feels in your self or how the other feels. Stay with the knowing in your heart. Explore what you really do know in your heart and what the other knows in their heart. That will change your sexuality.

Q: What would you say to a couple that have a sense or a feeling about this, but are not as yet defining that path for themselves? Where and how can they start this journey?

B: Where can they start? It has already started! The deeper discovery of what actually is already in movement is to be honest and true and not be familiar with your self or with each other. You must look at each other with a fresh open heart, a fresh open body even though your self goes, "I can't do that." You *need* to do it because when you first met, you weren't familiar, you were open to the exploration of your calling, of your union together and you were in the enjoyment of that discovery. By and by you got familiar and you began to use your self to have sexual experience, to have the other for your self and no longer for the joy of discovering the mystery of each other. You have to return to the mystery.

Q: I love that you say this because there is so much talk about tantra these days and my feeling is that a lot of it is just a bunch of rubbish!

B: That's truth! It *is* a bunch of rubbish because tantra is so much more than having sex. Tantra is the realisation that the entire movement of the universe is the pure sexual movement of light moved by the pure sexual pure beingness of what Consciousness is. There is nothing but tantra here. The part about the genital area is just one part of what this is really about.

You and I being here together are being love right now. You and I are in the enjoyment of the communion of our hearts with our body. That is a radiance of pure sexuality.

We are knowing love together that fills the space of this room and we are enjoying that together with our bodies in our hearts in our being. That is tantra.

The Genitals - Profundities Of Consciousness

Q: Why is it for a man and a woman that when the genitals are connected, there is in that sensation that 'extra feeling', which I think in the western world we don't see in the holy light that it should be seen in?

B: That's because the genitals or what might be termed the root chakra are profundities of Being, profundities of Consciousness. They are not just sexual instruments. They are profound Consciousness of a depth of Being right at the very point in which the universe first came to being.

The phallus and the vagina are actually profound intelligences. This is why when you bring the bodies together and man comes anywhere near the vagina, it is possible that the phallus radiates the consciousness of what is deeper than the man, of what is more than just his body, more than just his sexual appetite, more of what he is in the deep.

There is a response to that in the vagina that is more than the woman, her sexual appetites or her need of a relationship. In the response, there is openness. Somehow the phallus finds itself within the vagina and the vagina finds itself holding and being one with the phallus. Right there, union is already taking place in the deep. The phallus and the vagina have taken the shape of the powers inherent in the phallus and the vagina.

In India you find the yoni and the lingam are worshipped for what they really are, for they are not man and woman. The phallus and the vagina don't belong to a particular man and woman. They are profundities of Being.

The profundity of a beingness of pure sexuality equals love and equals light. That is what they really are. It just looks like they are on a particular man and woman, but they come from the Source itself.

We have this idea that they are for procreation or even recreation but what really is, is the fact that the Masculine and Feminine are already one. The Masculine and Feminine are profundities that spill out of Source, the 'I Am' or the Pure Self. They activate what Consciousness is and what sexuality is in the making of the universe.

That is our calling, to discover this in the making of love. It is a profound state to make real love. One can discover that the phallus and the vagina are much more than genital areas. They are profound levels of Consciousness that when aligned with the heart, have an innermost response and open up more than just our bodies.

Q: You said yesterday, "When you're tired of sex that's where lovemaking begins."

B: Yes, that is right. You discover that having sex doesn't fulfill your heart or your being. It doesn't really come into your pure body, which is your pure radiant sexuality. You are left hungry, hungry for more. When you are touched by a deeper level of meaning to make love and let your life fully belong to that, it awakens your body, it awakens your heart and you are fulfilled by a level of Being that matches how you make love. Union begins to happen. Literally your heart begins to realise itself and you awaken into love as love. You will see it shining through each other, a whole different thing. This is all real. It has to be gone into to discover it.

35

The Making Of Love Is The Revealing Of The Divine

*"Lovemaking is travelling into the deep,
all the way into the deep."*

Q: Could you speak about the difference between making love and having sex?

B: When we make love, we are prepared to give up our known life. We are practicing an openness that doesn't reference the past, doesn't reference whether we are going to get what we want. All that is let go of. It is knowing we are called in the moment to truly deeply meet. It is a meeting of God or Source within each other and yet transcends the other. We become one.

Making love is falling into each other's mystery. It is the discovery of the true connection of a heart meeting as the Masculine and Feminine. In his reaching into her, he is not frightened of losing his known life. In her opening to him, she is not frightened of losing her familiar forms. The making of love then is the making of the divine - a bringing down of what He is and a bringing up of what She is with no self-concern. It is saying: "God can take over. The divine can have us both. That's all we want. We are going to commune into the deep, show each other our deeper mystery by sacrificing our known lives." It is no little thing we are speaking of here. In that reaching in and opening up to the deep within each other, we are literally beginning to know and *be* the beingness of the place-less place we both come out of. We begin to know that together.

It's a clear: "Yes, this is it!" We know that this is 'it', because the self begins to empty of our hidden self-considerations. Most people believe this is a problem and should not take place but it is supposed to happen! We are supposed to reveal our self to our Self, show the limited idea we once moved by to our mystery.

We need to make love so cleanly and clearly where we are not just seeking comfort by putting our bodies together or having sex for pain relief or even as a habit. We are giving all that up. We actually 'make love' as in 'creating' love. We enter the divine realms of our being, enter the mystery of the Feminine, the mystery of the Masculine, enter our God-hood. It is not for self-satisfaction but something that we love to come into.

We meet our fear in this. We know when we deeply love each other the shadows come out. Love reveals the shadows so we can know our self and the shadows can be met by the light that has called us together. We have to fully be given to that! It has to have profound meaning for us. We will go through more difficulty than we did when we were just having sex but we will awaken to divine love that is being made even when we are not laying our bodies together. Now our sexuality is attuned and aligned with our divinity. We just look at each other and divine love is being made, the forms of our love are being made.

Our sexuality is the divine energy that turns the light of Consciousness into manifestation of Consciousness. We can truly change our life together, even the world together, manifesting divine Man and divine Woman. This is not just an idea. The living of this takes courage because we will be going through the eye of a needle by having such a deep calling.

Q: *This going through the eye of the needle is the coming up of the shadow, the seeing of what we have held onto. I know from my own experience that this can be really painful in a relationship. We can really judge ourselves for the messiness of what comes up. It requires a lot of love to keep opening in that process, to keep bowing down as all this starts to reveal itself.*

B: We were not told how this would be when we held hands as a little boy with the little girl from next door. We had this infinity together, where he just wanted to know her and she wanted to be known. We had an intimacy together that was most delightful, sweet and real. Once sexuality gets added to that intimacy of Being, we are in a different game altogether. Now the responsibility to manifest that sweetness starts to be available. Our love begins to unveil our self to our self and we see how we still function from how we believe man should look like, woman should look like, what we should do to each other and how it all should happen.

All these concepts of man and woman are the shadowy places in our selves. When we are really called to a deeper love, a love that is profoundly meaningful, we are willing to allow these shadows to come out. They do and will come out, because in divine love the body is emptied to be filled up with the new level of love or Consciousness that we are diving into together.

Shadows are coming out right now on the planet, the shadows of many different levels of the self that we have constructed. There is no difference between what takes place around the world and what takes place when a man takes on a woman and a woman takes on a man. Man and woman are actually the bigger scale. When a man takes on a woman and a woman takes on a man, we are talking universal! The dark and murky levels of the deep unconscious come up to meet the lights of the divine that are flowing in to transform, to transcend and to include. This is profound mystery. Even the shadows are the mystery.

Q: *I get the sense that it is the surrender of thinking that we can make any of this happen, whereas really it is about allowing God to do this through us?*

B: I am very clear that the God you speak of is our essential nature. It is not a hierarchy or some 'other place'. We are playing the game of being a man, of being a woman, but really we are of God.

We make little of what we are until we are really ready to die on the level of our self to a deeper calling and meaning to have a body and to relate to one another.

As a man to dare to look her in the eyes, dare to head towards her where her shadow may come out at any moment. He believes he is looking at the light of a woman and then comes the blade, or the axe or whatever it is because She is going to invite man to be so much more than limited, if he is to approach her. There has to be a total claim, not for his self but for the divine in him and the divine in her, so that the emptying out of the shadows is making room for the new. The shadows want to come home, home to the light that man and woman first saw when they were being called together. We have to grow the ability to allow this homecoming, through softening, through opening, through being true and honest to each other.

Our life together is not about comfort zones or about getting more manifest things. It is about diving into the mystery together. We cannot dive deep into the mystery whilst we are afraid of what it might reveal in our self. We have to let go of that fear. Both man and woman have to let go of the fear: "Will I get a broken heart?"

36

Sacred Worship

"Intimacy is a holy temple. Woman is a holy temple. Man is a holy temple. Your life together is a Prayer."

Q: Can you speak more about sacred sexuality?

B: Man's phallus is the divine shaft of the Masculine, climbing. Woman's body is the entire cosmos that revolves around this shaft of pure intelligence. It is not a man but pure masculine power tasting the beauty and wonder of the Feminine in every moment. The power of the Masculine and Feminine makes and creates all of life and it is developmental. It is the Alpha and Omega yet has no beginning or end.

On every level on the revolving spiral, there is a different entrance to the body-mind. When you get up to the top, there is still body-mind but because you have reached higher in the shaft and therefore have more light, this higher frequency begins to change the body-mind.

The higher you climb the more intense it gets. The Feminine begins to match the Masculine and vice versa in ever-finer frequencies of what is Masculine and Feminine Self-hood. It just keeps climbing. If woman does not invite herself to be open and speak to man when he does not climb, then everything jams up and we create a global situation, such as what we have right now on this earth.

In truth, all there really is in existence is the yoni and the phallus. This is the Masculine and Feminine energy. You, as Being, are climbing the shaft of light whilst you are enjoying more of the feminine fragrance. Every part that you climb begins to demonstrate in form more of what that frequency is, until through the love of God, you both reach the most high. You cannot speak about this; it is unknowable.

From this point comes a flow of nectar that comes all the way from the highest mind in both man and woman, and radiates the purpose of life on earth. All forms begin to glow.

The sacred worship of you, God-man and God-woman, is not to get familiar, not to see each other as something you own, but to see each other as the very nature of God. There is no fooling each other. You are learning to go through to the next level. You begin to make love in a more profound place, which reaches and changes the world.

In the making of love what moves man towards moving into a woman is his profound consciousness. There is no self in it. It is just this roar of a calling. It is a roar yet in it there is a fineness where she just goes: "Aaaahhh!" She feels it enter her and in a singular moment she can know the entire spiral and it downpours into manifestation.

She goes up into the most high of her Feminine, the most high of her real being and it can come down. Who knows how far she will travel through that spiral because she is travelling through the vehicle of his shaft of Consciousness manifest as the phallus. The spiral is her yoni and the heart-connection with her spiral moves in her heart, not in her mind.

Man's pull is to be true to the place where he is entering in his shaft. He comes up the shaft and this will have a relationship with a place inside the Feminine. It might not be all the way up, but wherever it is, it will definitely be beyond his previous experience with the Feminine.

Even if he has been with the woman for twenty years, it will be in a new place. It will be the offering of the embodiment of that new shaft, the new Masculine as a new man and the new spiral, the offering of the new Feminine as a new woman and the union of those two in their consciousness.

There is a possibility of realisation of the 'I-Consciousness' as man and woman in their union and in themselves anywhere along the shaft. Self-realisation can take place at the most profound level. Each level can be reached and integrated through their making of love.

When love has been made in such a way, man truly sees her from a placeless place. He sees the whole of her body with that that is seeing beyond form. There is no sense perception in it and yet it includes sense perception. There is no self in it and yet it is including self in the knowing of her beautiful form.

It happens the other way around too, because she is beginning to access his beautiful form, his formless form of the consciousness that is knowing her. She begins to be seen by something beyond the senses and to her that is God. Her form responds and expands and the possibility of that manifesting through her energy, love, her worship of what she is experiencing in and beyond the man, can manifest. His worship of her form and her beauty from the consciousness that he is seeing with, is the possibility of giving that energy direction. A new life can radically begin.

The making of love is essential on this planet. As we begin to evolve and we are in this attraction to God through the calling of man and woman, the testing point of how we are really evolving is proven in the relationship. When a man is truly beginning to be free Consciousness, able to sit deep and penetrate the world as it is and the form of his woman with the power of what he really is, he begins to open up in places in the universe that she has in her body.

I equate woman with the entire manifest cosmos and the seer of that is the Masculine. The play is that once man and woman begin to let go of their boundaries, the journey of true sexual intimacy and true evolution of Consciousness begins to happen. A man begins to discover through the loving of the Feminine through a woman, the deep mystery that is inherent in the Feminine and in a woman's body. Through a man's selfless loving of her, he begins to gain entrance to places within the universe that have to come here through his action, through his creating what that place is that he entered in the woman.

When this man makes love to a woman, she opens up another aspect of the cosmos. If this has not happened then there is something that man has to look at. He did not give her his all in truly undivided attention. She begins to open up places that even she did not know she had in her. He may experience a place in the cosmos that has not yet come into human intelligence. That is Cosmic Consciousness. She may or may not realise that place. It is dependent on the consciousness of the woman and man. This is the mystery inherent in our attraction.

He begins to know that the woman he is making love to is far more vast and mysterious than just a body or form. She has an immense mystery inside her that can be discovered. This is the possibility. That place begins to move and inspire him into sharing more forms of universal truth, universal love and purpose.

In the same manner, a woman can enter the Unknowable through the Masculine Consciousness. She begins to go up in his stream, which is her Masculine and discover the beyond. When the two are in union and are sharing this and bond to that place, love becomes known as eternal.

The Masculine and Feminine are already one, but that has to be lived *here*. If you play the linear game of sexuality, you cannot enter those places because you do not have the key. If you give up the linear through true discernment of heartfelt love, knowing and unifying for this alone and not for the separate sense of self, your person begins to be ignited with the great love that you already are in the deep. You become a transformed individual. This is the potential of real love on this planet. This will grow a different humanity.

In Conversation With Woman

Oh soft kiss
Like a warm breeze,
passing through my soul,
Is it you Beloved?
Is it you?

Come, come, again and again,
until I awaken.
Awaken me dear heart
I beg you.
Do not pass me by!

For I now hear your sweet song.
I taste the nectar of your being.
Oh! Beloved return me to the hive
I so wish to be alive
Alive! Alive!

You come! You come!
You come! You come!

My heart is but butter
Melted in your embrace.
My mind a thousand doves in flight.
Beloved! Beloved!
How could I have ever left you?
I lay forever in the silken chamber of your heart.
For, I now know, only upon your breast can I truly rest.
Only in the love of my Lord God
Am I truly Free.

37

Calling A Deeper Man

"What woman really wants is a man who could not care less about his ego or hers. She wants a man who only cares about profound love, intimacy and deep, real connection."

Q: *How can a woman call a deep man, one who really longs to go through the kind of deep journey in intimacy?*

B: How does woman call this frequency of deeper man?

Man and woman are in the making. They are not made. There is no end to the possibilities. They are always in the making and can never be complete. There is always more for us to be made into the likeness of our divinity. That is our joy! Who we are in the deep is complete. Utterly. It is eternal.

How woman calls a deeper man is not through the use of her sexuality. It is not through the use of her self; this brings further distortion and pain. Your hearts must belong to the truth of your own being, the knowing of what you know to be true at the core of our heart. You belong to that. That's where you bow down, that's where you kiss, that's where you take your body, that's what you give your life to, that's what you do. You give to that and cease expecting him to turn up. He will turn up more than likely not when you expect and probably not the kind of man you expect. You have to let go of all that.

Woman calls a deeper man in living more deeply herself, where she gives her whole heart, her whole body, her whole life to what is more than just her self. It is her own authentic calling to be love and to be true. It is her beginning to really recognise that she is already love, she already belongs to truth, she is already one with that. She starts to reorient her entire life to simply being love and simply being true. She does this in terms of her creativity and in terms of how she functions in this world. She doesn't live her life to pay the bills, she does what she really loves to do. She brings her heart and creativity together.

She begins to trust that who she is will bring precisely what she needs to be able to fully live on this planet. She is giving up the need as a woman to survive. She realises she doesn't need to survive for she already is eternal love and she has no need to convince herself of this.

She truly deeply knows this is the truth and is aligned with this in any moment. The universe naturally works to bring man and woman together who are on this higher plane of calling to be intimate in their loving of God, life or love together. It will begin to happen but don't wait for it to happen. Marry your own heart, marry your own life, marry your own innermost by living more honest to your heart's real knowing and calling. Change your own life. Live more deeply and he will show up. Don't wait for him.

38

Woman Can Call A Shallow Man To Keep Her Forms Intact

"Woman can choose a man who will not ravish her empty all the way so she becomes full of light. She can choose a safe man who will listen to her ego and not dare to step beyond what a woman wants personally."

Q: In my last relationship, although there was profound love, I felt like I was a teacher to him and we were not equally diving deep in the same way. I wasn't getting the same level of presence from him.

B: Let's have a look at what you are transmitting. Woman can purposely call a man to her who is not deep enough, because she wants a relatedness to the Masculine but at the same time she still wants to hold on to her forms of identification with herself as a woman.

I am talking about a very fine thing here, our ability to control the manifestation of life to what we want, because we are manifestors, we are creators. What we give energy to, will manifest at some point, sooner or later, because we are destined to know ourselves as Source and as creator. In that, we are also destined to know our human self, our self of self-identification. We must know our self to know the Self that we are.

Woman is quite capable of calling a man who will not challenge her. She can call a man to her who needs teaching, like she would call a child or a little boy. She can do this.

She can also call a man who is going to claim her totally, who is going to take hold of his heart and take it all the way into her body, all the way into her mystery, and so open her, so claim her that she doesn't know herself anymore on the level of a body-mind.

She is knowing a level of the mystery of profundity. He is going to go in so deep that in that claim she is changed. The change in her is as if she travels from the mystery he has moved into. She is in the light of it but sooner or later she lands back in the human self, she lands in her self and it doesn't quite match where she has just been taken.

There is a fight in that, a fight between the place he is taking her to, which is so profound, and the limited sense of self. She doesn't think it is a limited sense of self. She now identifies with that place and her self that is born and dies. She thinks that something is going wrong but what he is doing to her is taking away her comfort, taking away her forms, which she believes are real.

He took her to a transcendent place and this is going to cost him how he knows himself. For him to do this, he has to really be unafraid of what she might do. He has to be unafraid of going into her and claiming her no matter how her self reacts. He is still profound. He still loves her and sees her although her actions don't demonstrate the mystery she has just been in.

A woman who is not ready for a total claim will call a lesser man to keep her comfort zones intact. When she is really ready, she is ready to die to all the comfort zones she identifies with as likes and dislikes. She wants the Masculine to claim her fully, no matter what the cost is to her self, her person and the forms of her relationship. That is a big calling. When she is ready for that, He will come.

She must discern whether he is that, whether the man that comes in his man-form no longer belongs to his man-form and yet has seen it all. Such a man relates to the body as a vehicle of expression of his divine Consciousness. His body comes from the Feminine. She is manifesting his form in order for him to manifest his consciousness.

A man should not teach his woman but demonstrate love and truth and a willingness to feel everything in his body, as she does, whilst remaining in the deepening Consciousness.

Everyone draws to their selves whatever they want to experience or they let go of their need to have control of their experience and say, "Almighty, come to me! Deep man come to me! Woman who is ready for this kind of love, come to me!" There, the divine work can take place - the transformation of human consciousness and of the human body into divine perception, movement and great loving.

This is radical. You can only go as far as you are available to go. The rare ones go all the way. When I say 'go all the way', you are not going with a particular man or a particular woman. She, the divine Feminine, is behind every woman and He, the divine Masculine, is behind every man. Every man and every woman evolve to whatever level they evolve to in the Consciousness of the divine. The work is to manifest it by belonging to it, by living it, by breathing it and being prepared to die an extraordinary death to the belief that you are bodies and minds and that you need any form of comfort as the demonstration of love.

Let Him come and melt all your ideas away, let Him come and claim them, let Him come and hold your hand whilst also cutting it off. Let Him come along. Let your Feminine come along and do the same with him so that you are so honest together that the only hand you want to hold is the hand that is reaching into the divine of you and him. Anything that needs dissolving can dissolve in your honesty and anything that needs to come forth can come forth without any fear.

Your life has already prepared you for this moment but if you step back as a woman, He won't step towards you. If you step back as a man, She cannot step towards you. If you want to step into the divine, take the step. Prepare your life in each moment in how you relate. Let your direction belong to the heart. Always let it be of the heart even if it is not comfortable. You are preparing the way for a manifestation of oneness.

39

A New Belonging

"She comes all the way up on every level until she marries Him, Consciousness itself. She seeks her lover. She seeks Him. When She meets Him they are in union and they flower. The realisation of Self is the marriage of pure sexuality and Pure Being and all of life is the display of that."

Q: Can you speak about the energy of sexual desire? My knowing is that I don't need to have anything to do with it. As I sink deeper I encounter more sexual energy. It's a churning, like a constant motor. I want to understand the integration of this, because in its primal force there is a sense that it is Shakti but I don't fully know what that is in experience, but that is the word that comes, Shakti or life.

B: You are speaking of the primal force moved by Pure Being. Wherever Pure Being moves into primal force, the primal force takes the shape of or shapes what the being is. Hence, we love the universe because in us it moves as a form of expression, whether it is the stars, the planets or our humanness, it moves or opens in us the One.

When Pure Being moves through pure sexuality, then the sexuality belongs to Pure Being and forms Pure Being. What you called Shakti is the display of Consciousness as creation. We can also say, when pure sexuality moves not attached to a sense of a self or a person, then the being naturally comes and merges. But when the sexuality belongs to a perceived person, having a perceived self with a perceived need, then that energy moves only to satisfy a sense of self that is an illusion. This force is known in very much the same way as Awareness-Knowing, but the knowing has been attached to a body-mind person that has a beginning and an end.

The life force is then moved or distorted by Consciousness as a separate sense of self. When this is known by You as Awareness knowing and realising a deeper sense of what you are, the manner in which sexual energy was moved in your belonging to a perceived person, will undo. You will experience this.

As You, Awareness-Knowing, appearing to be a woman, stay and abide in the deeper knowing, you will come upon a longing that pulls you out of the desire for self satisfaction of any nature.

As you awaken to belonging to your being, by being true to it, you are mastered by your being. You are not doing this as a someone, as a man or a woman, you are raised up. You become a higher woman, a deeper woman. You are raised up into levels of Consciousness in the heights of what the Feminine is, what the Masculine is, towards Self-realisation. As you stay true and abide as Awareness-Knowing to your being, your being undoes and moves the sexuality up into Self-realisation.

Stay true to your being and your being is the doing. It is not doing things, it is just being what it is. In being what Being is, pure sexuality follows it and merges and true forms are birthed such as the cosmos, microcosm and macrocosm, all the same.

Stay true. Realise that in your self forms you will experience great vulnerability until You, as Awareness, truly remain planted in the heart of true knowing. The true desire is to realise the Self or what the 'I' is. You will experience great vulnerability in your sexuality, great vulnerability in your body, in your mind, in your self because in giving the power back to your heart, back to your being, all the power is removed from how you used to move sexually, mentally and emotionally. You will feel vulnerable on the levels of the body-mind but opened in Being. Remain opened in Being and Being will pour the pure into what used to be your old ways. In that, you awaken but you must remain and abide in being true. There will be levels of your old force coming up, power that you used to use to get what you want. All that will become undone.

Q: *It seems that life brings situations that are triggering egoic sexuality in its most fervent form. I see that I am still driven from that place.*

B: You are changing the driving seat. Now you are being honest to your heart. Your being is in the driver's seat. There is a change over in what you are belonging to, even though the imprints of old behaviour come up. They come up to be met by the new levels of realising You, Pure You. They must come home. They are levels of you that will always belong to what you are, so they come home in this, old levels of sexuality or behavior that you used to cover your vulnerability over with, for instance, the vulnerability as a child coming into puberty or it might have been the feeling 'I don't belong here so I use this, that, or anything to quell this feeling that I shouldn't be here', or 'I need to drug my sense of self in some way', or 'I *need* to have this experience'. They are levels in the psyche that Awareness or what you are laid down, deeper feelings that are unmet. In themselves they don't move your sexuality, your empowering them is what moves them. When you awaken, you come upon levels of deeper feeling that you have not connected with and met, but now your deeper communion with a greater knowledge and greater presence calls you to realise what you are, which is the Self.

Belonging to that with total response brings the feelings you have been avoiding intimately up. It will look as if, in moving deeper as a being, all that you didn't want to happen is now happening. Everything is coming home for you are the light of pure Awareness that makes everything real. You are the real, You, Awareness-Knowing.

Those feelings will come up. I point the way to allow them to come up, not mentally but directly as knowledge. The more they come up the greater the sense of your vulnerability because you have been suppressing them for so long. As they are met by You, as Awareness-Knowing, as a being rather than a someone, all that you are meeting is what you once gave form to. As you meet them, those forms will dissolve into the presence of your pure Awareness for in 'being met' they are returned.

What are those levels made of? Pure Awareness is what they are made of. On their return, they dissolve. By not meeting them, you are burying them in your experience to arise either at physical death or the death of your belief that any level undoing in you can ever be more than what you are. It never can be. They are simply levels of experience but you are the ground of all experience, Awareness-Knowing - I Am that I Am.

Q: I get the sense that it is about making an absolute commitment to that place. It's like a fire in there and even though I am meeting my past and layers and layers are coming up to be met, they never fully resolve.

B: Who is this that is meeting the past? Don't get confused here. Perceive deeply, clearly and rightly. The 'you' you believe yourself to be in the past, is not what you are. Let go of this idea that what you were in the past is what is going to meet those levels. Come deeper. Come deeper than believing you are a 'someone'. It is not necessarily going to feel good. If you need a particular feeling that you believe tells you what you are, you are never going to meet those levels of subconscious energy.

What you are, your being, doesn't need anything to change for what it is to be what it is. Your trust in that knowledge, in *living* that knowledge, returns you to your being and not your sense of self. You can delay coming home, but the ground of you *is* home.

The moment Awareness uses one thought of a 'someone' in the past, it begins to abide in the past, it begins to tell stories instead of abiding in the present where there are no stories. The entrance to what you are is in the presence of your knowing the Self or knowing as Awareness. Your sense of self will get uncomfortable as it empties out but you are abiding in the deep without needing anything to change.

You go through 'the eye of the needle' very quickly. Go through it. Come home. Use what appears to be time, which is really the opportunity to realise wisely. Come home when called. Why hang about in the past? Come home in the present. Stay aware, vigilant as Awareness opening as love, not trying to make things change but realising the truth. Be open to the return of who you once thought you were. That return, although it seems to be pain, is the door to what you are, thousands of doors within your experience all leading to Self-realisation. Take the opportunity. Don't tarry. Don't hang on. Open the door. Move in and all will be given.

If you don't open the door, don't move in, you cannot have as Awareness what is your inheritance, what you are. Move in. Step in. Discover what is in there. But you can also stay outside the door for as long as you want.

Q: Should I just leave it all alone?

B: Yes. That is exactly what I am saying. Leave it alone but consciously move deeper. Whenever those impressions come up, let them come up. Let them be felt. Let them be known but don't do anything with them. In not doing anything with them, they will return but they will only come home dressed as you perceived them to be at that time. Now perceive them to be welcome friends. Let them come home. Open your arms. Let them come home.

Q: What you're saying is that I really don't need to keep making them anymore. There would be a part that is no longer invested in that way.

B: Yes, it is an old investment but in realisation there is no investment because you are not going to gain anything or lose anything. You are returning to the realisation of what you are, the Self.

As you respond as Awareness to pure Knowing, you know Pure You. That is where your joy is. That is where the happiness is. That is where the abundance is. The abundance is you.

As you abide in being true, there is no old form. There is only the moment of newness and all form there is made Now. Known Now to be the Self, there is no separateness between Consciousness and its forms. All this is made of the Self.

Return to be the Knowingness that knows the Self, then you can see the play of life, all of its gifts, all that it brings. Even pain or disturbance is a gift to know your self and what you are undoing in your return home, the return of the old relatedness to a new belonging.

Timeless Awareness naturally forms the phenomena of the expression of Pure Being. Such is the cosmos as one whole Being. It is all in your own life, infinite doors opening to the greater mystery of you.

40

Attraction Leads To Aversion

"Only the light of love will free you.
No form of man, no form of woman will free you.
They are simply manifest mirrors of your deepest knowing.
Walk into the mirror and merge into the light!"

Q: I find in my life experience when I come into sexual relationship with man, I lose my capacity for unconditional love. As a single woman I know this love but when there is attraction involved, I become very identified, very emotional and very stuck in that.

B: Attraction is always about your self. In attraction, there is an attraction of self wanting and needing, of self like and dislike. When you are attracted, there is always an aversion. Attraction leads to aversion. You will have a like and a dislike and that is always about your self.

We are intending to change the consciousness in this between man and woman. It is about the calling of the real. In a calling, your heart calls you. You long to melt into deeper Consciousness with or without man, with or without woman, be it with a flower, with the space in this room, with people, with the planet, with the universe. That is your possibility. You do long to return to that directly, where two bodies with totally different energies and varying consciousness of the Masculine and Feminine Principles, can become one because the truth is, they are already one. Their attraction and aversion makes them two. To stay with the truth, you will be awakening to the One but everything that you put into your attraction and aversion will break open. This is why you don't want this when you still belong to your old self.

We are bringing intelligence to this calling. We are bringing intelligence to this to know that as we are called to be deeper, this will activate the higher levels in our consciousness and will activate the deeper levels in our body. It will also activate the old patterns to empty out so they can be filled up.

If you are called to share this with man, then share this with man non-sexually. It will be your sexual energy but it won't be lodged only in the genital area, it will have all of your body. It won't be about an attraction to get something. It will be an acknowledgement of who each of you are. You will pass through each other to a certain level.

In everyday life, this shows you what is to be developed, not as a problem, but out of a movement of fulfilling your true calling to incarnate and to open the deeper levels of your consciousness and the deeper levels of your embodiment so you can truly know who this 'I' is with no end.

'I' will be calling you to really know your self on deeper levels so that you know that when sex is an attraction, it has something to do with your self. When there is a true meeting, you won't need to move into sexual engagement. There will be a deeper meeting, it will just be about the meeting. If there is an alignment for you to come into some form of partnership together, then there will be a deeper calling.

You have to really belong to the deep of all this otherwise you simply keep moving back to your self, positive and negative. You have to be clear that when you come towards each other, you take each other on. Taking each other on means, the other will be allowed into all that you are, all of your self, all of your body, all of your consciousness. The exploration is for you to move into the One consciously by not being two. Anything that is two will come up for the One to know as the both of you.

You will speak less about your day, "How was your day, darling?" You will speak of, "What are you opening to? What are you knowing? What are you seeing? Isn't this amazing, when we made love last night, my love, you took me into such an unknowable place and I began to know the unknowable place, but I can't quite put it into words." So you wait for a while and just enjoy being in the anticipation of the more, and suddenly he or she says: "Yes, it's this!" It takes time for it to have form. There is immediate presence, immediate activation in your union but in terms of its movement in form, that takes time.

It has fine form in the inner. If it is to come all the way out, the whole of the universe aligns with what you are connecting with and it begins to form. If there is any level of you that you still want to keep, it won't actuate into form. It will be twisted and distorted.

When you really begin to come together, you belong to what is to take place in the evolution of all of your bodies opening to the more. Your lovemaking will be entirely different and your belonging will be a belonging to each other's depth. This is not a one-off thing, this is something that has to deepen. It is never about you as a self, it is about who you really are.

Your real enjoyment comes from what is next, not what is here in your present relationships or in your past. It is what is to come. Move into what is to come before it gets here. Move to the high domains of your next level that you are entering into. That makes it have form. In keeping your forms as they are, the new levels of you can have no existence. There is no marriage.

41

Knowing And Feeling

"Man tends to enforce knowing but as a self.
Woman tends to enforce feeling but as a self.
When man and woman both embrace Knowing,
the profundity of what you are
as the Feminine and as the Masculine,
comes through freely.

This is where your joy lies,
in your melting, realising oneness.
It lets loose all your hidden forms.
It lets loose all your stagnant ways of consciousness.
It lets it all loose so that you can know your Self."

**Q: Knowing and feeling, there is confusion around this in
me because I strongly identify with feeling. I associate that
in my experience as knowing. I am not quite sure what is
meant by knowing as opposed to feeling.**

B: I am going to put this towards woman as I am speaking to
woman. When woman feels, unless she belongs to truth or
the depths of what the heart really is, she relates feeling from
her self. It is all about feeling in her self. That's a recipe for
pain because your self is divided. It is not you. It is what you
give form to but only for your self, not so that your being,
the beingness of what woman is, can flow through a self.
You don't need feeling to indicate how things are going.

Woman associates feeling to how things are going, "He loves me. He loves me not." If he really reached you, you would be blown well clear of feeling. You would come directly into the essence of who you are – She, beautiful, pure innocence, so sweet.

When your feeling is an expression of what your heart is knowing to be true, it is no longer about your self. Whilst you need to feel good in your self, you create the bad. As a self with likes and dislikes you create opposites. Who you really are has no opposites.

When the Feminine shines through you, there is no opposite of feeling. It is always the Good for She is love. When you relate as a particular woman, having particular likes and dislikes, which are all based in your self, this will keep your sexual energy only in the genital area. It won't cascade through the entirety of your consciousness and your body. You will relate to feeling good or feeling bad and you will relate this to anything you do, even the weather, and the weather of your man.

The place I would call you into, is to relate to what you most deeply are before you relate to yourself as woman. When you relate to what you deeply are, it is not conditioned by a like or dislike. It is the Real You. It is Her. It is You. You cannot make yourself go there. This happens naturally by you functioning from your being. This makes you a deep, radiant woman.

There will be times when you move back into your old functioning as a woman, trying to get something for your self. In that, you keep all your forms intact. You believe this body is you. You look into the bathroom mirror when you paint your beautiful lips and put color on your beautiful eyes. When you do that, how much do you do that for the woman you believe yourself to be? How much do you paint on conditioning? Or are you painting on the yet to be realised, the yet to become? Are you painting Her on? Do you see Her? Eventually you will let go of the image in the mirror. You will be knowing Her. You are so much more than an image or a particular form.

When man comes along, if he is true and deep enough, he can reflect this in a moment. He comes along to realise who you are in him, thinking you are out there, so he can say to you in a moment, "You are beauty-full! Do you see? You are full of beauty!"

Begin to differentiate between self like and dislike and the Real You that is love. Nothing can touch the Real You. It doesn't need any protection. It doesn't need any make up. It is who you are. It doesn't need to have a particular feeling to know it is what it is. real.

See whether you are relating to feeling as a knowledge through your self or whether you are relating to knowledge direct, which gives you a true vibrancy of feeling. Know that. The true vibrancy of feeling will not have you making 'other'. The vibrancy or the feeling of a self will. In relationship with man, feeling with your self will make your man separate from you, but you are already one.

The radiance of this universe is oneness, which is the Masculine and Feminine Principle as One Self. There is not two here. Whenever you are feeling and you are pushing man away regardless of his weather and his garbage, you are making him an 'other'. You are seeing him through your self. Sex and love then is for your self and not for your being.

For you to be this clear is for you to return to love as your own Real Self. You can then be with man. The whole of your heart and your pure sexuality can open without even needing to make love. Love is being made in the seeing, in the knowing and the being together yet you can make love and watch how the making of love from this place has no want and need. It pours into each other the knowing of the Masculine and Feminine.

Everything begins to open up. You begin to know the universe and transcend it in the same moment. You will shed everything in your forms of consciousness and body that you have been identifying with that cannot go to where you are headed. It will all be opening up on its return back to nothing.

42

Union When You Are Not In Partnership

"Regardless of whether you are in a partnership or not, you are in relationship with the most high, the most real, the most deep having living universal forms."

Q: *When woman doesn't have a partner but still there is that yearning for the union with the Masculine, can this process of awakening happen even when you are not in a partnership with somebody you love?*

B: Most definitely! You are making love with God or with the Source. It is truly like that. BE the body of the universe making love to the power from which the universe comes, which is Consciousness.

There is a marriage going on within all of us whether we are with an outer partner or not. We are in an inner partnership moving towards re-union in our innermost Self.

Yes, this can certainly happen in a woman's life who belongs to the depth of her heart. In her being true to what she knows, she is in a deeper place and she will transform her self into the likeness of her divine womanhood.

Often this brings about a reflection of that process within us outside, particularly when we are attuning and are aligning our life with greater truth and belonging to our hearts. It is the very dance of love that we are talking about.

43

Her Light Invites Man To Be More Than His Self-Experience

"When you remain open, Woman, you have radiance. You are the radiance that lives every thing and relates every thing to the One.

When you are straight, Man, you are such a vast no-thing moving from nowhere going to nowhere. That is the direction of all life.

In their marriage is transcendental power and goodness, light and love nourishing every being in the planet. Everything is evolving and there is nothing to do there as a self. "

Q: When you speak about 'taking a man on', 'taking a woman on', I have a question around her willingness. Will it awaken the light in him or knowing in him?

B: Your light always invites man to be more than his self-experience. Your light invites him to be more deep, more real and more meaningful from the moment he sees you. It invites him beyond the parameters of his separate sense of self. It says, "Come! Be divine because we are already one."

It is this that awakens his heart. It awakens him to what he really belongs to and his meaning of having form, which is to infuse the forms of his life with the love and meaning that he is.

Why does he incarnate? Why does he have form? To bring his full consciousness endlessly into this life and to share that with woman, to recognise woman is his other half, to live a fully embodied life and to incarnate his deepening growing meaning in life. You inspire him to do that. He recognises in you, in your beauty, in your wonder, in your mystery the possibility to form the eternal in a moment he gazes at you.

44

Loving Deeply In Spite Of His Self

"Do you soothe his soul, my love? Do you love him that much, he who is Him? Do you soothe his soul from judgment and the ridiculousness of thinking he is judged by the Great One who is Himself?

Soothe his soul, soothe his heart with the great love that you are. Soothe it. This is your growing capacity, to give the world your soothing heart resonance of love, for You are She. "

Q*: There is a deep longing in me to be met, to hold the hand of divinity and move towards it in relationship but I have attracted a partner who says: "I don't understand your vocabulary. I get uncomfortable around it." Is that mirroring back to me my own fear or unwillingness?*

B: What is mirrored back to you is that the man doesn't belong to you. What belongs to you is your knowing that you love that man. *That* belongs to you. You know you love the beingness in this man and he is being formed by you. He could not manifest without your energy bringing it into form. Sounds bizarre but it is the truth. Your love of him is so much more than just the self. He might say whatever he says at whatever level he is at, but if he really is your man, which means you love what he is, then you love what he is in spite of how he comes across to you.

Q: Is this a choice one makes?

B: It is not a choice. It is an immediacy of your heart. It is the light of your heart. Choice comes from a level self that you are developing for you are the Feminine Principle developing the forms of self-hood. You are blazing those forms fully with your light of love.

He invites you, consciously or unconsciously, to be all that you can be in your body of love, to open your body of love. You know you love him. Does he really need to change for you to love him or is it simply the truth that you love him at the core of his being? Remain in that love then you can open that love through knowing your love. You can love him while he is asleep or reading the newspaper or watching sport. Whatever it is, you can love him. This is totally different to what the world would teach you.

Q: Is it the Feminine that sets the barometer of love?

B: My way is to simply *know* love, whether you are man or woman. My way is to know love at the level of the heart in spite of what you believe your self to be, a man or a woman.

We are Conscious Awareness appearing as man or woman. Although we are speaking about man and woman, the Masculine and Feminine, we are really speaking about manifesting that that we already are in the deep through the love or calling between a man and a woman. This is the same as saying form and formlessness.

Your barometer isn't set by your wants and needs for comfort or for love. Your barometer is what you know to be true in the depth of your heart. If he doesn't seem to be responding to you, what has that got to do with whether you love him or not in the deepest place?

If you looked in the level of your self that you as the Feminine Principle are evolving, you will know the level of self that you need to transcend and include in your love. For instance, you are seeing his self and it doesn't match what your self wants but does your love know him? I would say it does. Simply love him no matter what he says.

Q: To allow that love, is that to invite union or to experience union?

B: It is to realise that that is already in union. You are already in union. The man sitting over there reading the newspaper who seems to want nothing to do with you, he is already one with you. If you open to the truth that this is the case, you will find that this will open in him. If you are just taking on the belief that he is a body-mind sitting over there and you are a body-mind sitting over here, then that belief will come true because you are the manifestor of the universe.

If you really know you are love and you stay open to this love, you may find the miracle that shows you that you are already in union. This calls him to awaken. Don't take things from the surface. Look deeply into your heart and see what you really belong to and relate to him from there.

45

Woman Yearns To Be Made Love To

"Woman, in the love of man in the heart of hearts,
you are giving him permission to enter your body
and make it new.

Man, in the love of woman in the heart of hearts,
you are giving her permission to completely
enter your consciousness and take it deeper and higher.

She creates a new body, a new life.
He creates a new consciousness that is able
to move that body forward.

This happens in both of you, for you are one.
It plays out as man and woman.
You become aware of the greatness of all,
awakening deeper and deeper to the purpose of being called
as man and woman to heal The Tear."

Q: I have been on a journey with a friend of mine working together with a spiritual body of knowledge focused on the marriage of the polarity of the Masculine and Feminine. It was never a sexual relationship. During this process a man came into my life where we deeply explored in the body. So, I was having the spiritual experiences with one man and I was intimate in the body with the other. I knew I loved him and I knew in the moment I met him that he represented for me absolutely everything I feared of the Masculine coming in. Can you give me some insight here?

B: If your life or your calling to God or Source is towards the union of man or woman in the movement of your being in sexuality, then woman wants to be made love to. She wants to have the kind of intimacy where man is able to reach from his consciousness into and through his body into her body and into her consciousness. That is the making of love.

She will not be so interested in having a 'spiritual man'. What she wants is to be made love in the spirit. She wants it physically. She wants the transmission of his being through her sexuality. That is how the universe is manifest. The transmission of Being, moving through sexuality creates the universe. That is really what she wants.

This communicates what woman is, what man is and makes it manifest. It also opens up the consciousness of both man and woman to the deep. It opens them both up to the formless. This is what the making of love really does, deeper intimacy of our being moving through our sexuality. They are able to reach into more than their body and sexuality. Within that, their sexuality begins to expand and they begin to know as the beingness of woman, as the beingness of man, an embodiment that is deeper than the bathroom mirror image they see.

They are now able to access more of what manifestation is. That is really what she wants because then she is in touch with a deeper body that does not pass away, she is in touch with her body as the divine Feminine and she is also in touch with the divine Masculine having a body in his transcendent state. He is in touch with her transcendent state and yet it has a body, it has more depth and an intimacy that transcends the world and yet includes it.

Now their relatedness is far deeper than just 'man and woman' yet it is blazing through a man and a woman. This is really what we all want when we are interested in God through tantra. We want to know that what we are is shining throughout the universe both in its fullness and its consciousness.

Q: There are ascension teachings on the planet that say we are ultimately going into the light and 'out of body' and yet we are still here in the body. It seems like there is a transpersonal process going on. Somewhere in me there is a conflict around this.

B: I wouldn't say it's a conflict. I would say it is a knowledge, a knowledge awakening in your feminine heart that light is a finer form but light is the *first* form. The light of the Self is a form. The light of the Self expresses this light in various frequencies all the way down into manifestation.

As we awaken to this light, having our form, we also awaken to form being the light. When you speak about ascension, the ascension to me is quite simple: if man sees the light of the Feminine in woman, he is drawn to love, he is bringing the ascension down into form. If woman sees the light of the Masculine in a man, she is bringing up her form into the ascension. That is the marriage point because the light and its forms are the same One, the Masculine and the Feminine are that One already. That is the Self.

You are interested in lifting your form into the light. He is interested in bringing light into form. You are the same One.

When he doesn't want to do that, he is afraid of bringing his light into full incarnation in form, because he knows that staying in the transcendent realm is far more simple than bringing that that transcends form into form. It is here, that the real work takes place, the real awakening of what spirit is or what light is in the forms of the multidimensional relationships we experience on this planet, where every being is at different stages of the evolution of consciousness and form. Right here is where we can be one with the great One, together *as* that One.

46

Love's Calling Knows No Conditions

"All that you have to do is be true."

Q: *You spoke of the Feminine needing to relinquish that sense of comfort and there are a whole lot of ideas that we have as to what a relationship should look like around monogamy and commitment. A man can come towards a woman yet he may be in relationship with another woman and yet there is love. How does that translate? Is monogamy a requirement or does none of that matter if it is a deep journey? I get confused about what unconditional love is.*

B: I am going to bypass this in this manner. Why be interested in the conditionality that the world has presented? Why not be more interested in the communion, knowing and belonging to what deeply comes to you. When we don't have self-consideration, we can hear a calling so much stronger than any condition of 'it should look like this' and 'it shouldn't look like that'. When love really calls you, would you turn away because of a set of rules? I suggest that you wouldn't. This leaves you open to the discovery. This is what life is about, what man and woman is about.

Listen to your heart more than to any conditional idea about how it should be and you will step beyond the norms.

I am not suggesting that the relationship should remain 'one to one' or not. What I am saying is follow the calling of love and know it in your heart and your whole body. Listen and belong to that calling no matter where it takes you. Otherwise you are going to restrict the un-restrictable, contain the uncontainable and try to own the un-ownable. Dare to love that much that you belong to the Beloved no matter how He or She calls.

47

If Your Being Says "No", Don't Go There

"When your self belongs to your heart and deeper, you will find that your body can be, know and speak the truth of love."

Q: I am deeply exploring the energy of my being with a man. He and I are exploring what it is to be in sacred partnership. I feel like I am coming undone in this process of loving and I am confused by the concepts of polyamory. I feel this love for the creation of love and also in how it sits with me in my heart. I am being very cautious.

B: I don't advocate polyamory in my teaching. I am not saying it is wrong. I just don't advocate or teach it.

If polyamory doesn't sit in your heart or isn't one with your being, don't go there. There will only be pain in it. Pain that is 'just for pain' has no worth whatsoever.

When one is being true and goes through pain, that kind of pain has profound value because love then is not about your self, it is about that that is deeper than your self. When we head towards a partnership and we experience pain and we go through that pain rightly, we open the doors into another place that heals where the pain comes from. There is such a thing as having unnecessary pain.

Only go to where your being is called to go. Don't go against your being. If your being doesn't want to be with a man that has another woman, don't go there just because a part of your self thinks that it loves him or wants something from him. Be very clear that you actually belong to your being and love between man and woman must be an integrated movement of where his being and your being want to be together. If that is not the case, don't go there. Don't force this.

Q: It feels like his being and my being are drawn together naturally on many different levels.

B: Sexual intimacy that is pure and real doesn't have to involve putting our bodies together because our bodies are already one. I understand a part of you loves this man on other levels but we are talking about integrating what you are as a woman and what he is as a man in a deeper place. This has to be a calling from his being and your being. Be very clear about this, particularly if the man has other women. You really need to see whether this is true for you or not.

Q: I don't know how to do that. I am not clear with it.

B: If you are not clear with it, don't go there. It is so simple. Don't go there. You will return back to your heart space and you will call a man that is not for your self but for your true meeting of divine union, love and partnership. Be patient enough to call that kind of man. If you were a man, I would say, be patient enough to call that kind of woman. You have to be clear what I am speaking about has to be the realignment of his being with your being. Only go where your being goes in terms of your deepest intimacy. If you are not clear about it, let it drop.

Q: We have been having such beautiful intimate experiences. I don't want to let it go.

B: You can have beautiful intimate experiences but can a man totally give up everything else to be with you? You can have beautiful sexual experiences but can a woman totally give up everything to be with you? If there is any use of sexuality to *get something* from another, there is a distortion in it. It is not utterly true.

Be called to fully integrate what you are as the Feminine Principle, what he is as the Masculine Principle, to fully integrate that consciousness into your heart and into your body. Any man that is escaping a deeper connection with you will only use you for the pleasure of having your body. Although you may have beautiful connections sexually, they won't be able to go deeper, because it will still be about your self. Turn everything to be about and for your being so that you become wholly integrated to what you are as the Principle of the Feminine, the Principle of the Masculine.

Your confusion is only because you are not absolutely connected with the deeper place. It is still about your self and his self on some level. You can go on any amount of ceremony but that is not the reason to have sexual intimacy with another.

Sexual intimacy is belonging to the Great Being that I Am in the deep. When it belongs to this, it means life is called to integrate all the separation in self back into the heart, back into the deeper places. You will need to be truly intimate and engaged on every level of life as man and woman to bring that about. Otherwise, when other partners are involved, you can use sexuality to escape giving the All to each other.

We have to cease using sexuality to avoid emptying out our self. When a man and woman come together and they are not using anything to hide anymore, this begins to undo their selves. If it is not truly a deep calling, leave it alone.

This is a radical message and it will reach anybody that can hear this. When a man and woman truly come together, they are not using others to hide away from what they are meeting in their relationship together. They can't use another to hide from the process of self-emptying and integrating a new level of consciousness. They can't use another to have a safe harbour in. They are giving all to the relationship. This is very difficult to do when others are involved in sexual intimacy because the self can use this to have a rest. In that, it is ruining the possibility of a finer intimate connection and a real integration of the higher dimensions of life into the body-mind of man and woman.

In Conversation
With Man

Love's Longing

In her fullness she came,
bursting from the nowhere, the now-here within me,
immediate, radiantly in her full dancing form
she shone before me.

Enticingly she drew me to know her,
experience her shifting light forms.
Deeper and deeper she sang me into her woman,
her womb of life experience.

Manifest me! Manifest me! She cried out loud,
Experience me! Experience me! She sang out loud.
Burn for me! Die for me!
Do not let go! She screamed.
Until it is done, when you and I are one.

What could I do but hold her tight
in my burning arms of passion,
Until she and I burned no more.

As quickly as she came, she disappeared.
Did she ever exist?
Was I just dreaming?

48

A Man Is Made New In His Death

*"The only death you are ever going to experience
is the death of the illusion that you are a 'someone'."*

You are the transformative light of every level of
consciousness, right the way into form. By you just having
existence, you have the growing ability to bring other
dimensions of greater reality into embodiment but they are
never for you as a self, a particular man or woman with a
particular name.

There is a greater reality moving in this reality and from this
place you can say, "I am this man" and it comes out clearly
that you are this man but this man is beyond what this man is
in his sense perception. You have this experience of him
being so much more than his body-mind. In fact, you realise
he is 'no mind whatsoever'.

When man is no mind whatsoever, woman becomes a
flower. When a woman is truly about budding and flowering,
she is what She is. She already *is* this. She is a constant of
this but She is not a particular woman. She is the totality of
the Feminine, the pure Feminine. If you dived into the
Feminine fully, you would die as a self and you would be
reborn as love. She is a continuum of flowering.

In truth, this is what every man wants in meeting woman but
he cannot bring her to flower whilst he believes he is a
particular man with a particular self. He cannot flower the

Feminine from any pattern of lack. He knows if he heads towards woman from his true innate power of pure consciousness, which is not a power *over* but a power *given*, his self and the forms of his self will die in reaching her.

He has to trust that he is pure, formless consciousness and only in his death will his forms be made new by the light of the Feminine. Only in the death of his old consciousness is man made new. His self dies in his belonging to what he knows in the deep, not to a static truth.

The worst kind of man to a woman is a man who is static in his truth. If his truth becomes liquid and he lives his liquid truth, she will also die for Him. She will die to her old forms of life and cross over to the other side of the galaxy to be with Him and create new forms of that partnership. She forms a relationship of the partnership in forms of relating. He belongs to this too as She is the master of that in the highest level, He is the consciousness or direction of the partnership, and neither belong to a self.

In a true calling to love or truth, you become closely acquainted with death. Befriend it! Death is a re-seeding, not a receding. It is definitely the receding of your self for the re-seeding of higher reality. Allow death to give birth to new love and new life, which means Now. Greater reality is being birthed in you as Awareness, it is known throughout and your essence will vibrate: "I am Reality!"

49

It is Now Time To Drown

"Your love and your depth lie in the unfamiliar, in the meeting of the Unknown within you and within the other."

Q: My woman tells me she doesn't know how she can be with my aggression, with me being triggered again and again. This morning we spoke about how she expresses this. There are many weird and wonderful ways. Sometimes they are a direct hit, a kick. We laugh too. Sometimes it is too good to be true.

She calls me on a fundamental distrust of where she is coming from. In the deep, I do not doubt her. Yet she too lives out her self before my eyes every day in terrible ways. How do I know she is not just gloating, goading, baiting, ruling and riling me for her own perverse pleasure?

This morning I realised, "So be it, it still is the best way to trigger and kill me anyway. But then I do know and therefore must trust in God and the Lord and she and I know that Lord well.

B: Man, hold onto her as if she is a rock and you are in the middle of the ocean. Sink to the bottom remaining fully aware as you go down deeper. She is 'doing' what must be done without her doing anything. Remain fully aware in it all. No turning away! You are a great swimmer, Man. It is now time to drown!

You are inherently free already and form doesn't need to feel or behave a certain way for you to remain free. If man controls woman, he's telling himself and her that he is not freedom itself. But he recognises he is free 'somewhere'. She provides the space, form and experience for him to *be* that freedom in and as Awareness, regardless of the conditions or the polarities.

50

When A Man Loves Woman Like God

"When a man loves woman like God, his self is continually in death. Death brings him to deeper realisation. There is only the death of his phenomenal sense of self which awakens him to his power of consciousness."

A connected man enjoys the death with woman and also enjoys the awakening of Her. There is nothing more fulfilling than to have a woman in your arms that you are awakening to God with. It reveals what you are meaningfully together for, the revelation of the Principles of the Masculine and Feminine up to the surface as man and woman. When she reveals in such a way, it wonderfully breaks his heart.

He has always wanted his heart to be broken by the Feminine coming to the surface. He gets down on his hands and knees in praise of what has just taken place. It has made him new.

In the same manner, it happens to woman. When a man reaches her so deep, connecting her to what she is in union with what he really is, she is illumed by love. She is knowing union. They are one consciousness, one body, one movement. It is much bigger than their humanness. It consumes the entire universe.

51

She Says: "Meditate The Universe With Me!"

"Relate to what you are knowing and be true to that whilst moving in relationship with woman. Be true to what you know without pushing, shoving or juggling what woman gives to you to meditate."

The deep levels of you are the Masculine, not man. The levels from the deep up are the Feminine, not woman.

A symbol of this is the Infinity Symbol: ∞. It is a symbol of form and formlessness known by the only 'I' in the universe.

Mainly man pays attention only to the emptiness, woman pays attention only to the forms. Neither pay attention only to the Knowingness, which is the only 'I' in the universe. Quite a miracle is happening throughout the levels of You, Awareness, who is moving as Consciousness or Knowing and coming all the way to the surface. Otherwise you would not have a body right now.

All forms belong to the Feminine Principle. She relates form. That's why she loves relationships. She relates form to her deepest knowing. She relates all the forms only to the One. This is her potential. That makes her forms of relationship pure. She is the pure relatedness of the Feminine Principle. She knows it all belongs to the One, the Great Being, from which she springs forth.

The consciousness and the direction of consciousness belongs to the Masculine, not a man. He is that that moves from nowhere going nowhere, and in that action or direction, all the forms of relationship evolve to realise the Self.

It's a mystery because woman's tendency on the surface is to give man all the stuff she doesn't want to relate to. She says to man, "Take that! Meditate that if you can. I am not having this. You go meditate that and show me what's real about that." He says, "What are you going to give me?" He doesn't say, "Only give me what I want." He is the pure Masculine, he doesn't move away from what she gives him.

She turns in endless circles of life. Look at all the planets, they move in circles or spirals. She relates all the forms of creation for She is the master of that and the mover of all forms from light to solid form. She relates all the forms only to the One. She doesn't relate them to any sense of self or person; She has none. She is the light of love herself. She relates everything to the divine.

In her movement of life, she moves and as she picks up all the relatedness in her psyche, She passes it to him and says: "Meditate that!" She relates all the movement of all life and She knows it has to evolve, move and grow so that true forms of relationship in the universe and on earth, that match a frequency of depth and love, manifest.

She is a being that is moved by a mystery that even she doesn't know she is moved by it. She relates all beings in the universe and any gap between their surface experience and their potential. She brings that to you, Man. She wants you to penetrate what she gives you, her consciousness, with your profound depth. She tests you to see if you have any depth and if you believe you are a man-form or Pure Consciousness. She gives that to you and puts it into your hands. She is always giving you the next level of your relatedness but it is aligned with the earth, its populace and with the universe. This is *big*, not small. She relates that, gets hold of that, and somehow it ends up as how she moves.

We are all evolving and raising up the deep to the surface and returning the surface to the deep. That is the calling of man and woman. The goldenness you experience in each other is not the man-form or the woman-form. The goldenness you experience in the man-form, in the woman-form, is beyond form. You have to have had enough suffering to give up the idea that He or She is outside of you. He is within you, She is within you, already one with you. He is a pure frequency of light and goldenness. She is a pure frequency of light or goldenness.

You name him on the surface but He is in the deep. You name her on the surface but She is in the deep. You don't exist on the surface but the light of what you are comes up and forms the surface, because you want to know each other all the way in glorious form. In the deep, you are already one and you want to experience that frequency of Being in form.

The only death you are ever going to experience is the death of the illusion that you are a someone. The illusion that you are a someone is also a real expression of what you are in the deep. What you are endeavouring to do as a being is to come all the way to the surface and give form to what you are without any distraction, without any covering of your heart, in full openness. You want to experience what you are, which seemingly produces two, but man and woman are the same one in two different principles, Masculine and Feminine. They are seeking each other right now in form to dissolve in the deep pleasure of knowing they are one.

If you are willing to die to your sense of self, for the love you already are and relate it as two that are really one, then you are being prepared for a very rare revelation of God as man and woman. Whilst you as man seek her for sex, for self-gratification, and whilst you as woman seek him for your self and even to control, then you will keep being disappointed. Give up the seeking and return to your heart and live it. Listen to your heart and respond.

In this response, you begin to see from the deep all the way to the surface and you are in constant revelation of the divine. She is saying to him, "You think you are a form but you are not a form. I am forming you! You are formless knowing me. You are the formless eyes of pure Knowing knowing me. What makes you think you are a body? Meditate the universe with me!" She keeps bringing it to you until you get this.

Suddenly you are so open in your heart and deeper that she gives you something. She awakens to you, to what you are in the deep and your light comes right the way up and penetrates every level of her form beyond her sense of self. Now she is knowing you from a new level of her body. Her body is opening and freeing up, her heart is opening and freeing up because you now have a consciousness that is able to go beyond your and her sense of self. She loves that.

52

Taking Her Through

"She must keep bringing the relationship of the universe and its evolution to you to meditate through your consciousness and through your body."

The Masculine Principle is really nothing. He is constantly giving up his form to the knowledge of his formless nature which moves him deeper into form but from a formless perspective. The form then gives itself up and comes through.

As the Masculine, man begins to take what is coming through. If he does not take it all through because his intelligence is not up with the speed of his consciousness, he will measure what it is costing him as a man. That is limitation because he is not a man, he is the profound state of the pure Masculine. When He moves into form, that is the same as making love, that is the same as placing a man's phallus inside a woman's yoni.

He is literally moving into form and completely moving into the Feminine. He wants to know who She is. He wants to go all the way inside but he cannot get all the way inside of her and reach her heart centre, which gives up all her energy back to the Innermost, if he is counting the cost of how much he should love her.

It might cost him a thing or two in the mental, emotional, physical realm, mainly in the mental: "Will I lose my freedom if I love her too much because she might get attached? I will not be able to do what I want to do."

We are talking about a loving that is demonstrated in form, a consciousness that is constantly moving into form from a free state of Being, therefore creating new form, a consciousness as form that is constantly giving itself up into the formless. That is the very nature of the Masculine and Feminine, of Shiva and Shakti. She being the surrendering principle, He being the penetrative principle. He becomes Feminine, she becomes Masculine in the trade off. She begins to enjoy the formless nature of consciousness that makes her whole form radiant because he is moving into her formlessly which creates new form.

New form is the Feminine that is coming from a man's gift of being truly masculine. The new formlessness then is masculine through woman's surrender of moving into that place. There is a total trade off. The Masculine Principle inside a woman gets integrated. The Feminine Principle in a man gets integrated. He is now knowing the Feminine in his heart, she is now knowing the Masculine in hers. This grows both form and formlessness. This is a real partnership. There is love and love is nothing, which means everything.

A total union means no separation. There is just this brightness that is experienced as, "This is good. This is beautiful. This is wonderful." There is an ease and within that ease, He moves to her and She opens to Him. In that moment polarisation occurs, they become absolutely divinely two and the cycle begins again. New realised form happens, new realised consciousness happens and again they come to the bright place of beautiful nothing.

53

Are You Available for Love?

"When you are true, Shakti is enormous.
When you are not true, She shrinks.
When you are true, the power of Knowing is vast and deep.
When you are not true, it is little and puny.

This is how the universe works.

Shakti, the pure feminine power and energy
only reveals Herself for one who is aligned with truth.
Truth is her lover,
the one She really belongs to and moves for."

Be straight, powerfully radically raw and honest, so you can know whether you love and whether what She is reflects your love. If you don't know, you will be powerless in love's movement, powerless in past movement. You need to go to the truth.

Can you move to love beyond her self even as you go through the gate of her self, even as you go beyond into her love? She has a self but her mystery is beyond her self unless it has embodiment.

The embodiment of her mystery is what you are about. Consciousness of your mystery is what she is about. The relatedness of what all this is, is what she is about. The orientation of all this is what you are about.

Is she really not available or have you not been available to her? Did you close down because of her self?

In that case, she will have less trust in your availability of a depth of consciousness to be with her while her self moves. You don't want this to be seen. You are divided in how you can reach her, serve her and be with her. You have a preference for her self to be easy, which means you really want to keep your self as it is.

If you really want self-transformation and to open to an enlightened perspective of relatedness to what God is in man and woman, you must expose your likes and dislikes of self, to you through the woman. She will show you exactly where your likes and dislikes are through a level of self that may open. She is moving by it.

She demonstrates in many ways that your body is a formation of her and that when you are clear about your deeper consciousness, being that that moves her into form, then it won't be about your response or reaction to her self. It will be her response to knowing you love that within her, which is love. Your consciousness is reaching beyond her self and reaching the light of love that drew you together. She wants to feel your depth in her body regardless of how much self that releases.

She wants to know that you have the depth of consciousness, so when she reveals her self, you remain in that depth. Otherwise you are quite an ordinary man who is not called to a depth of relatedness that moves the stars, evolves consciousness and is the light of love moving.

When her self moves, how much of her self is known in your body, in your self? If you are not able to bring all your consciousness into your body, how can you bring it into hers? You have to move by a little bit of heart-knowing to be with her. Then you will be able to reach the heart-knowing in you, in her.

She tests you to see whether you are deep enough to be able to reach her, knowing that if you reach her in the deep, it will release her from patterns that she has covered her heart with to protect her from a broken heart and to keep her forms the same. She will be willing to reveal all that she is as a self, to shine the light of her heart through that, if you are available to let her self pass through you. Otherwise she has to hold her self whilst she is with you because you lack the depth that she requires to open up to.

If you are really available for her, it won't matter how her self undoes in your loving. When you reach her, her self will undo exposing the vulnerability she covered up. For her to open to love, she needs to know that you are available to her love no matter how many masks come off. Are you available for her totally?

If you are her totality of consciousness and she is all your body, if her body is your formed consciousness and your consciousness is her formed body, you can give her your all right now. You could lose a great deal of your self over this but you will reveal what you are, naked, open and free. What you hold in your form, Man, is what will move in your woman as self. What you hold in your forms - thoughts, feelings, things, houses, jobs, ways of living, likes, dislikes, is the first place she will go to in your calling of her. What you hold onto in your form, she will display in her self.

Woman, what are you holding in your emotional body? What you think about in your emotional body, his profounder consciousness will reveal that to you. You reveal to him how he is using his consciousness to hold onto the familiar and he reveals to you where you are not quite available to completely let go of all your relatedness to your present way of life. You both want each other all open. That means you will pay the price of loss of self but that opens you to love, which is not for a self.

She knows when you are playing around, when you are not available to change your consciousness. When she is also not available to change her way of relating, then you both want to stay the same. You don't want to move into the unseen, into that that is unknowable. Only when you move into it, it will appear as the new.

You said she is not available, but it is you who is not available. What you are holding in your body and mind is what is displayed in the pieces of your self, interior and exterior. You cannot keep your exterior clear while your interior is not clear. One affects the other, they are the same.

You can be open to her on the outside but are you open to her on the inside? You can be open to him on the outside but are you open for him on the inside? Is form going to be recreated by a profounder state of consciousness or not?

Is it Shakti-Shiva? Or is this just about the same old continuance of the same old drama? Are you available for the profound power of the Masculine and profound love of the Feminine? Your past will get totally blown away and as it is blown away, you will experience the hurricane of it until it turns into a breeze.

54

Adoring Her

"You can love a woman in such passion of adoration that even in the looking at her, the mystery of the universe is present in your experience. In the making of love with her, you enter Her, into the vast universe, into the cosmic mystery She is."

When a man makes love and he is truly making love, he is loving his woman at core. He absolutely adores who She is totally. The field of adoration is so utter that he has to see her and that is enough for him to open so deeply and go into her. I am talking about real adoration here.

When a man is adoring who She really is and is entering her, he will enter the patterns of humanity as a whole - patterns of himself, his family, her family. He enters the patterned subconscious. You will go through this, Man. That is your greatest gift in the making of love. Your greatest gift in making love is not just having good sex or even having good love but it is your capacity to move through old fields of patterned energy without turning back. Do not turn back, carry on in.

When you come to a place of a greater love of God within your self, it begins to happen naturally that the draw towards your woman is very much the same as your love of God or Source. Your love of truth is also your love of form, your love of woman. There is no longer a difference between going into the emptiness and the embrace of the total form of

She appearing as your woman, appearing as your life, appearing as people walking down the street, appearing as the whole movement on this planet or in this universe. It is endlessly vast. Your arms then are not just embracing this woman, they are embracing the bigness, the openness that She represents in your heart and beyond.

This has you going through patterns and by going through those patterns you are literally taking them on in consciousness. On some level, they are being meditated or opened in your masculine consciousness. Through this, you open to a much vaster light of Her, a much greater depth of You.

Your battle in this has to do with your trust or knowing that She is your love. If you do not know that She is your love, you will not be able to trust your love in you or in her. In the same manner, she must know that you are her consciousness. She must be able to trust your consciousness, otherwise your relationship will be very rocky and shallow. She needs to trust your consciousness.

In many ways, the Masculine and Feminine movement as man and woman on this earth is the endeavour for woman to be open and to remain open, and the endeavour for man to be trustable on a level of consciousness. When man has a depth of consciousness, she equates this to her love of God.

This is the play that is always shifting and moving in bodies, in forms, in hearts, in minds, in the Masculine and Feminine. It is around the trustworthiness of his depth of consciousness and the love of the greater form of woman, the greater form of life. The trust that all this, tsunamis, earthquakes, you name it, is still great love. The trust that your depth and where you are moving to is coming from a limitless source of truth. This is what is going on between man and woman.

A man who is beginning to realise this in his depth, can just look at his woman and open her up to her invisible love-light nature. She can just journey into it because he looked at her. This can happen. *That* is great sex and great love.

If you experience great sex and great love, you will also experience great death. It means that what needs to leave your psyche, whether it is mental, emotional or physical will begin to die. It will begin to dissolve and your ability to allow that is you being God-conscious.

You can have incredible experience in relationship, in a mere reflection looking at her and the light of you going all the way in, in her opening or her being who She is and that light coming into you. You can enter the great mystery together but this will cost you your familiar sense of self. It will show up in your relationship and far, far wider. This is consciousness knowing what is next to transform and making space for what is next to come. That is what your relationship really is about.

55

Her Mystery Does What It Wants With You

"Man, be the catalyst that heals your woman's shadows and calls her into her full radiant light. This is your healing!"

The universe represents woman's mystery and this planet is one of her mysteries. This is why, Man, if it is your calling to know woman's mystery, her mystery must have every way it wants with you. Her mystery is allowed to touch you, move you, have you, do what it wants with you.

In your endeavour to find God in woman or as the Feminine Principle in the light of her heart, She makes you available to meet her mystery. She doesn't know this. If she knew that this is taking place, it could be said that there would be a movement of self. But she doesn't really know her mystery.

To realise woman's mystery in her nature of being God as the Feminine Principle, man might learn that he cannot have her for his self, because He is not a self. He is Consciousness taking on man-form, a form supplied by the Feminine Principle.

If he really wants to know her mystery, he needs to learn to drop into his. His mystery is to not move as a self, to not move from wanting her but to remain in the heart and experience everything that she supplies in her mystery.

If he willingly dies to really know her, see her and realise he is already one with her in the deep, this awakens his deeper levels of consciousness. He has access into her mystery, access into woman's mystery by selflessly reaching her. She loves him for that. She loves him as God in masculine form, not his self, not the name he gives his self, not the address he lives at on the outside, but the living presence of him being available for her mystery to do whatever it does to him. If he stays in the middle of that without moving any level of his self whilst moving his mystery into hers, this awakens the deeper level of her body. He is then able to access the deeper level of her body by being more than just a self.

He might have gone through quite a bit of pain with woman in his life. He may have built self-defenses and wanted to taste her for himself but realised no fulfillment lies in having woman for himself.

The Principle of the Feminine is not available for his self. She is totally available for what he is at the level of his heart as her man, already one with Him as He is already one with Her in the deep. The love of woman in this manner awakens his mystery of God within himself. When both her mystery and his mystery are moving, they will be knowing God, the deep, what love really is. It won't be of their selves or of this world but it does enter their selves and enter this world through his revelation to her, of who She is.

She loves him for it though it is not always demonstrable at times when her mystery is moving. If he wants her for his self, he won't hang around. He will go and find a woman that is not available for the mystical life of love and willing to die for the love of He that transcends all space and time now, appearing as a possibility in this man that says, "I love

Thee, I adore Thee, I long to meet Thee in the depth and I won't run."

Whether we are wearing a man-body or a woman-body, a man-form or woman-form, there are many levels of this body. This is the domain of the Feminine Principle for She is the light and power of love and energy. She is the maker and mover of form, but she only moves it for Him. She does not move it for a self. He is the power and love of the light of the beyond. Truly they are already one. He is not really interested in form. That is something he is mistaken that he enjoys. He enjoys what She is, his primal state of love that came forth out of the Self, just as he has. He is available to fill her up with dimensions within her body that she has no idea of, no idea that he can bring what she is out and flower and how she can flower his heart beyond any sense of self.

They will pay a price for this kind of love. It will be their selves. They will go through the experience of death before they physically die. They will go through the experience of self levels that they never really found any fulfillment in, yet clung to with all their might.

This world is actually built out of this, the stuff of our 'clinging' or holding on. The earth isn't. She is very much in the endeavour to bring about God-man and God-woman, supplying the energies for God-beings to inhabit her.

56

When Man Needs Space

"When man does not fully acknowledge that She is his innermost love, he will not go all the way to claim Her because he will fear the loss of his space. When man begins to be the free consciousness He is, loss and gain are no longer his concern."

When man needs space, when he already *is* space, he is in the wrong place. He is not available for her phenomena.

The basic space of phenomena is the forms of sexuality moving from the lights of basic phenomena of Awareness. Awareness moves and light is created as Consciousness. The phenomena is She. Consciousness or space is Him. If he needs his own space, he has confused space with a particular room and confused form with something other than what is coming from him. If he stays open, spacelessly spaced, she can move her phenomena in his awareness without him needing any other space.

He will die to believing that form and forms of relatedness with woman can imprison him. He won't need to go and find his own space. He *is* the space in which she dances her phenomena. If his space is confined to his self, she will be too much for his confined space.

All this is known by moving more deeply and meaningfully into the heart when relating. It is simply revealed. Take the woman to be 'a woman', rather than the brightness forming the reality of Consciousness that is the space of all phenomena, the Awareness that is the background of all, and you will believe you are a particular man and a particular woman. Actually you are Awareness knowing Consciousness that is radiant, free and spacious. In that space, all phenomena - the bright lights of what She is dance, displaying every level of her body. Pure sexuality is aroused and moved by the presence of the basic space of what the Masculine is and he has no need to escape her.

57

Your Fear Of Past Hurt

"If you really want to love woman, let all the prisoners of your love free, Now. You will be made new."

Q: I am with a woman who lives two hours' train ride away and I know there is fear in me to fully be with her. Can we speak about this?

B: You are creating fear because of past hurts with woman. For you to hold the hand of a woman and hold her in love, you need to be deep enough and real enough to walk as a man of truth. Otherwise you'll draw to you a woman who doesn't want a deep man. She wants you to be two hours away because you're not deep enough to go so into her in your loving, in your being together, so that whatever comes out of her, you are deep and stabilised enough for that to be transformed in your body, in your heart, without running away.

She won't be able to trust as she opens to love that the un-love that comes out of the system is okay, that you won't run in the other direction as it comes out. When you're not after an easy time with her, you are meeting her in her essence even when her essence doesn't seem to be coming through. You're in the practice of surrendering, you're in the practice of self-knowledge and self-knowing so you know what you're doing with her. When I say 'with her', I mean in the meeting and in the relating. You know what you're doing. You're not propagating more fear because your lovemaking can put the fear of other women breaking your heart into her body.

If you have had a broken heart, let it do its work otherwise you will need another one and maybe another one and another. There is no woman that hurts you. I know this is a tall order for most people. There is no man that ever hurt woman. There will be some resistance inside that doesn't want this to be true. You want some woman to be responsible for hurting you. In the biggest or the smallest depths of what we are from, that's never ever happened. She's always been one with you. The pain is simply your denial that she's one with you.

You are here to leap into an entirely different level of innermost belonging and experience. You have to let go of the women that have hurt you. There was no woman that hurt you. There was only the Feminine that blessed you. On the level of self, I agree you can have that but you are the creator of real life and you are the creator that resonates real life from Being into form.

Q: Are you saying that I created that pain?

B: Well, you're a creator but what I was giving to you now was the bigger picture. You are the creator of the universe. its radiance is She. They are not two; they are one, the self-illuminating radiance of your Real Self as both Feminine and Masculine. She illumes the universe into form. He is the knower of it. They are one. They are not two.

Any pain you had was simply because you're being drawn or called to a higher participation in the universe, the universe of love between man and woman and their divine bodies, divine consciousness that is truly inherent in you regardless of what pain your self is in. The pain was a real blessing.

Let go of your self trying to identify the lower level of the man instead of the masculine power and potential to live in the man. Until you've let go this self-idea that some woman hurt you or you need to protect yourself against another woman, you cannot know love, divinity or revelation. If you let go, everything will straighten up. The energy of the pain of the moment that you're still identifying with, holding onto and keeping, disables you from loving woman more utterly and completely into freedom. The pain will go but it will come back through you because you're its source. If you're frightened of this, you're frightened because you think it's going to be painful for you. If you're not frightened of this, it really won't matter what kind of pain comes through your experiential cells, it'll simply pass through. Anything that you're holding onto will simply pass through. You must practice letting go. Letting go is Now, not at any other time.

If you really want to love this woman, then let all the prisoners of your love free Now. You will be made new. Do you know love with this woman?

Q: Yes.

B: If you really know love with this woman then nothing of self will touch that love. You will still experience the release of self in you and in her but if the love is true, it won't get touched. If the love is for your self, it is not real love. If the love is about truth, about meaning, and she really is a woman you are drawn to deepen with in the highest reality, communion and connection for you to know there is the One here as you and her, then go towards her meaningfully. It will release her ghosts and yours.

The question is: Are you deep enough to allow those ghosts to move through? That's what you have come here for, to allow those ghosts to go through and at the same moment not pay any attention to them while you are realising the next levels of the Real You.

Cease protecting yourself from woman. If you protect yourself from woman, you're protecting yourself from the world. If you can't love woman, you can't love what the world is for you. If you can love woman, the world will not be a problem for you. It becomes the domain in which you transform through your heart.

Where there is pain and where there is movement, these are places of learning. These are valuable to your evolution, learning and deepening. They are valuable. Treat them sacredly. Let them be the opening to a new place of value. See this is meaning in your life. If you really want to reach her, you can't reach her while you are holding the fears of past images and energy of other women.

If she is your woman, what have you to fear? If she is not, you have a great deal to fear because you won't be in balance. If she is really your woman, there is simply nothing to fear but plenty to learn and much to open to. If you use her for a holiday, use her just to have sex with and call it making love, it will grow in a problematical relationship. Move in the deeper you. That's what you are here for.

Discover what the deeper you is as this man. It will change your entire life not just this relationship.

Q: I was sitting with it then thinking there is something that I'm not getting. I would agree with you it isn't sex. I would say it is making love.

B: If you know it is making love then making love will definitely expose your ghosts, the ones you are still holding onto. It will seem in relationship that she is allowing you totally into her body but as Consciousness. You can open up more of her divine body than she can. Otherwise why would there be man and woman? If you allow her into all that you are as Consciousness, she will open up in you more consciousness than you can open up on your own.

There is man and woman because you are the same one appearing as two in different polarities. The opposite polarity can open in you more of your real polarity than you can; you can open more of her real polarity than she can. That's the whole point of this. She will open up your ghosts for you. Just say "Boo!" to your ghosts otherwise you won't be able to enter into deeper levels of what love is together. You will be barred from it because your beingness is not in the same resonance as what you are endeavouring to bring your selves to together. You have to have the same resonance to go into a deeper place together.

Q: In some ways, we walk deeper paths. I mean she is very much into emotional release work and being very emotionally expressive. I think you said earlier about love not being an emotion. Is it more of a sensation?

B: I believe you're going off somewhere. I'm here speaking and being truth with you. I will keep bringing this back to you and ask you: Is she the woman you can deepen with and move in life with? Is she the entrance to all your fears, all your doubts and all that you can be?

Q: Yes

B: She will have to be all of that. It has to be reciprocal for her and if it is, what she does in emotional release has no bearing in our conversation whatsoever. It's not about likes and dislikes. It's about the innermost connection that changes all that. It appears your parents made this body, this man. It appears you made this table or this carpet. You're relating to the belief that self made the bodies, self made man and woman. It's not the truth. Source makes all of this.

You should be interested in the next level and the next, and watch how it forms instantly. You are already moving beyond the form. You are in the nectar of the flower. You are not interested in the flower. The flower is beautiful but you are already onto the next birthing of the flower. You are the source of where the nectar comes form.

That's where your total beingness and enjoyment is, what is prior to the forms of this life. This is how new forms arrive here very naturally. Don't be interested in what she is doing, the emotion. She will either have you panting in emotional release or you will be loving the depths of what She is revealing to you because it is not the woman that reveals to you. Gently dismiss the woman. Acknowledge the Feminine that is holding the woman. Acknowledge the light of the Feminine. Her forms will change. You will get disinterested in her forms. They are too shallow, they come and they go. Be interested in Her, in that that does not come and go. This has you seeing Her, loving Her and also being Her.

This works the other way around too. If she is really what will transform you and if you are really what will transform her with no effort and in the enjoyment of beingness together, nothing should hold you back. If it holds you back, it is for your self. Anything that holds you back is for your self. If you are drawn to higher-level union as man and woman, let none of the emotional release stuff hold you back. Know each other's essence, love each other's essence. Enjoy the essence enjoying the universe, enjoying the deep, enjoying the profound. Reveal the profound to each other however that happens, otherwise you'll just be talking about your day. How was your day?

If your day is revealing the more that is not actually here yet, that is a good day. Otherwise you'll just be a robot. You'll be caught in the same old, same old, same old form. You'll get restless on the chair.

For unity to happen for you and this woman, really take her on regardless of your fears and doubts, then you will not have fears and doubts. Move into what is real, don't stay out of it. Forget your old life. Move into the real and you'll *be* the new life. If you don't move into it, you will be partial, and the old life and the new will flippantly pass through you but you won't be able to touch it or hold it because it doesn't belong to you. If you can be all of this with her while she lives two hours away, that is good.

It is really not about the man or woman in terms of bodies, old sexual habits and old forms. It is about the man and woman as principles of the universe knowing and responding to the heart of hearts as their own beat. Everything else will simply transform in that.

58

Transparent To The Deep

"This instant is the only instant you can be true to the depth of your real heart's knowing and become its manifestation"

Man has to be transparent to the deepest place he is reaching as Consciousness within himself. If he is not, he will block off the truth and knowledge of the moment and his ego will do whatever it wants to do.

As man and woman, we are used to cutting off the Source, the knowledge of love and truth that is inherent in every being in this universe. We cut off and go about life in a separate sense of self, even if we pretend we're not separate, even if we pretend that we're getting a bit enlightened.

When a man comes to a profound calling to the Feminine, he has to remove the steel shield that makes him invisible to his True Self, his deepest place of Consciousness. When he does, he becomes transparent to what he is in the deep.

He knows whether he is being true or whether he is twisting the truth. If he is truly in the love of acknowledging the deep within himself, it will be the deep that moves through him towards a woman. The deep wants to be one through that man.

59

Your Willingness To Take Her On

"Your depth invites her to open.
Her opening invites you to greater depth.
That is the tantric way.
The evolving marriage of openness and depth is true union."

Your Willingness to 'take her on' equals your willingness to be true to this life and your real possibility. Your willingness to take her on equals your willingness to take life on as it is on this planet and bring it to a greater place of love, rightness and clarity.

Your willingness to take her on equals your divine destiny. She is your Feminine Principle that is in the deep of you now having a woman's form. If she is that, you will be taking on her self as well as her heart. It is also the other way around. She will be taking on your self as well as your heart. That's the work. That's the bond.

If you want to keep your self comfortable, don't take woman on. If you want to keep your self comfortable, don't take the world on, don't incarnate. If you really want to meet this so that what you are comes all the way here and has relationship, move through your fear and take her on, fully. Discover with each moment, with each breath, what that means.

You will find this is freedom itself and the more of what you are will shine and deepen. She will be able to fall into the depth of you. She will be so open that you will be able to move into the openness of her. That is union.

When man does not fully acknowledge that She is his innermost love, he will not go all the way to claim her because he will fear the loss of his space. When man really begins to be the free consciousness that he is, then loss and gain are no longer his concern.

60

'She' Is Not In Sexual Experience

"In the union of man and woman, what really surprises man when he approaches woman from his purified heart and consciousness, is how he loves the deep of Her.

He cannot know Her if his sex is limited to his root chakra. If his sex belongs to the whole of what his heart is, transformation begins to happen. He begins to realise his body is a vaster opening of what her real form is.

This works the other way with woman. She begins to realise that her body can flow into the vastness of his emptiness and this changes all her forms."

At some point, you realise She is not over there, She is not in sexual experience. You are never going to discover Her in sexual experience and she is never going to discover You in sexual experience. Let me get this clear, never, never, ever! You are only going to discover Her, you are only going to discover Him, when the heart of your being moves through your intimacy. That is when She is there. That is when He is there.

She explodes or opens when Being is around. When Being is around She gives everything, when Being is not around she gives a pinprick of energy, a little bit of self-satisfaction.

When your heart is given back to your being in your intimacy, She will reveal Herself. It isn't the amount of sex

you have, it is you belonging to the truth you know in
Being.

Being shows you everything. In Being, all your energies
open because that's Her opening up. Sexual intimacy one
with your being transports you into all Her levels of Being
expressed in light and mystery. This is what is available
here.

You cannot do anything to make this happen. It would be the
same if you sat in a cave, die to your self and awaken in the
unfolding of the death that reveals who you are. There is
nothing to do but jump into the calling that draws you. That's
all there is to live for. Don't live for the woman. Don't live
for the man. Live for the calling. Live for the truth of Being.
Man and woman will come alive in that and realise.

61

His Innermost Love In Form

"We are one with the Beloved already. We are called to move in duality until some sparks of awakening begin to call us deeper and higher as Awareness having Consciousness, as man and woman, until we see a greater spark of truth and possibility.

We are here to unfold and unfurl our destiny as being one with God or truth. Our destiny is to land in our heart the Beloved, to land in our heart the supreme being that we are, and for that to have embodiment as man and woman."

When a man has a woman as his beloved in partnership, in a life to discover more God within and without, she becomes his innermost connection with love and his outermost manifestation of love as her beauty, her creativity, her shaping of her love into forms.

When a man chooses a higher-level woman, he can be challenged by her ability to bring form to her higher gifts, unless he sees her as his innermost love in form before his very eyes and responds to that truth with all his heart.

A higher-level woman brings her silence into living forms that serve God and all. A true man has gratitude for his love relationship with woman and is inspired by her too. Otherwise he will seek a lower level woman that does not challenge his status quo.

62

Loving Her As The Divine In You

"If he is to be unlimited, man must go towards woman selflessly. He must serve her selflessly. In this, he will discover those parts of himself where he is not selfless, as she will also in her opening and closing.

As he heads toward her selflessly, it is not so much about growth for him, which will happen naturally. It is about the growth of the Feminine as the universal expression of love. He is not trying to grow her, he is endeavouring to know Her and in knowing Her profoundly, the universe expands with more light and more love."

Q: Through my personal experience, I have come to realise that the making of love with my beloved is like a Gateway to God. In some ways, I have been blessed to experience this physical body falling away during the lovemaking, entering into this vast depth of blackness. Then the mind jumps in and identifies what this is and it just goes. I am just trying to get some clarity from you because I don't understand fully what is taking place. Through the lovemaking I sometimes feel really drunk. I have so much love in my body, I don't fully know what to do with it. I feel like I'm going to explode.

I feel the feminine energy during the lovemaking rising within the body and sometimes the masculine energy coming down. They meet at the heart and it is very beautiful. Sometimes the feminine energy comes all the

way up through the top of my head. I was just wondering if you could shed some light on what's really kind of going on there for me.

B: Where do you want me to begin?

Q: At the beginning.

B: When you said the feminine energy comes up through the top of the head …

Q: Comes up through my Kundalini through the spine.

B: We believe that She comes up from the base but that is not where I know Her to come from. It is a place within. A part of her rises up from that place but She comes out through the heart. You say she comes up through the head and you say there is a sense of being drunk?

Q: It is like a feeling of getting drunk but very clean. There is no heaviness, it is a light feeling.

B: But it is so much more than what you are saying. I don't fully get the experience you are describing that is why I am asking. I feel the Feminine rising within and the energy spiralling.

All round the world particularly in India, Thailand and other places in Asia, Buddha is seen to have millions of spirals on his head. Those are not spirals on his head, they are the radiant bliss of She. She is not just his head. She is his whole body. That is what She is.

When She seems to come up from what we think is the root chakra and there is a meeting place in your God centre, the crown chakra, She opens up at the crown. In the East, this is Self-realisation and you will see lights around the crown of seeming enlightened beings.

Have you ever seen an enlightened being where the crown is completely holding the entire body? Very rarely will you experience this because when you realise the Feminine, the Masculine and the One, this is what happens. She doesn't just climb up and illume your mind. She is the illumination of the entire field of creation. All those spirals are an indication of the multidimensional lights of the Feminine which is one light but it seems like there are millions of lights.

If She is making you drunk, you need to ground Her more. If you are with a woman you need to be meeting her, manifesting what this love really is so it doesn't just stay up in the air. It actually comes through your heart and there is a resonance of that beginning to take form. It begins to take all the forms of relationship and all the forms of your relationships begin to change because you are not getting drunk on her. If you are getting drunk on Her, there is something missing. You are taking Her for your self on some level.

In the total giving away of life as it is and as it was to what is God or to an increased opening in the heart of Knowing, in the giving away of life for love and truth, She rises and She is not a woman, although She can come through woman or even man.

When she came through what appears to be 'this one', feminine intelligence married the masculine intelligence. When that took place I was able to see into all worlds, on all levels, through loving Her so much as God in me. In that, She came all the way through me and not just in the head. She did not display mind, She showed me the entirety of creation that She embodies for truth. I was able to not only be fully in the total Awareness and Consciousness of the entire universe, I was also able to realise it as my real body that is Hers. Immediately after that, I began to realise beyond the Masculine and Feminine into God or into the beyond. My entire life changed.

My love of who She is and my love of truth gave me the eyes to see, to know and to be ongoingly intimate with the entire universe, which is Her. In my experience of that union, there was no other and immediately my life began to create new forms. I did not respond to the past whatsoever. I began to live what I knew in the immediacy in my heart and within this revelation. I began to *live* the revelation.

If that is not happening in you with the woman that you are discovering the divine with, you have not fully moved into her body as yet and she has not moved fully into your consciousness as yet. In other words, you are not the same one as yet. You need to move totally into her body, no matter what takes place. She needs to move totally into your consciousness, no matter what takes place. You will find a different life will begin to take place. You won't be getting drunk, you will be stone cold, cosmically sober, loving, creating, moving life forward, not as a self but as a being.

Q: That has already been revealed to me about the Feminine.

B: Which is what?

Q: Which is woman.

B: Do you think that She is just going to reveal to you once and that's it? No, for She's endless. If you are getting drunk on her, there is some level of sobering up that has to take place, the *living* of what is opening up in you. Otherwise you will emotionalise the love. It won't be unified in you.

Ask yourself if you are meaningfully moving your relationship and this life on? Are you still holding on to any conditional aspects of your life or are you living the fresh and new? Are you seeing and knowing her fresh and new and are you letting go of everything that needs to be let go of?

In this, you will enter a different sphere of consciousness having true form, a different sphere of deeper sexuality and deeper consciousness, different altogether.

63

The Radiant Presence Of His Heart

"In the making of love, woman's body registers to man's consciousness the openness he is entering into in his profundity of Awareness, registered in her deeper body as an open 'Yes' to his presence."

Presence is when I as Awareness begin to live everything of a higher, deeper nature and I begin to live those higher levels as man in my body with woman. Those higher frequencies move in an energy we call presence, the more we live what is next in our innermost depth, the more presence we have. It is the living activation of a higher order of universal love and truth living in our bodies. That is living presence.

What this does for a man is that sex no longer is something in his genital area alone. Sex becomes the radiant presence of his love that emanates from his heart. He is able to move in his presence whilst being in her presence and they become one living presence. His lovemaking comes into such a fine vibration that he begins to experience that his old ways of sexuality have no place in this new place of presence he is moving into. He can make love without the use of his genital area because he is making love as love in the fullness of pure sexual energy, which has all of his body. His sexual energy is not just concentrated in his phallus, but it is vibrant through all the systems of his body. He is in glowing presence.

64

Holding The Space Of Presence For Her

"Man will never be able to reach woman in her deeper heart through his conditional sense of self. To reach her, he has to be brand new."

The structure of the universe for you is your present experiences as a man, your present experiences in your relationship and what's happening there. Your relationship is the universe of experience. Your relationships are your universal reality. It is all there is in existence, universal reality of relationship with your knowing. That's how you change the universe. That's how it moves. It moves because you are relating to Knowing. If you don't relate to Knowing, your universe won't move. It will remain static and problematic.

The moment you relate your knowing to your heart, the universe begins to move and show its mystery. You begin to discover the way of opening the universe so you can truly see it and be in it as Awareness and as a deeper man.

The truth of liberation is to see that you are connected with every woman you ever lay your eyes on as long as you lay your heart there at the same time. You are in connection with the Feminine for She is already one with you as the Masculine and there is no separation.

Whilst you relate to your woman as a woman that is 'yours', you cannot clearly begin to see that it is the Feminine that calls you to be deep and true in her body of existence. You then cannot be true to your woman.

The pure state of Masculine and Feminine presence is of deep respect for each other as 'no other'. When you are drawn to a woman, it serves the meeting place of He and She. It has to be a bond. It is the giving of hearts.

A man enables his power of reaching the Feminine Principle in his woman by being profoundly, radically honest to his deepest heart level. He cannot be true to her as someone outside of him. He must be true to her in his own heart, because this is where She is. Outside She is in the form of that woman, inside She is the eternal presence of the Feminine moving with man as the Masculine, creating the universe, already one. She is not outside.

If you are familiar with yourself and familiar with woman, you will not be able to reach Her in this woman or in the Feminine of the universe because the only thing that reaches her is authenticity and the willingness to die for profound Awareness appearing as love.

If you are not available to die, you are not available to love. The death of you in a moment is your entrance into the mystery. No death, no mystery, no entrance.

The moment you bring your presence to the deepest mystery of her, you hold the space of presence for her to rise in that. She needs to trust that you can go into her and that her forms that empty out can still move in the presence of You. She will allow you in because she is beginning to know that not only can you reach into her but what spills out, you will meditate into freedom even though it hurts you in the process. Although it will disturb you, it will bring you to know a greater meaningful purpose to exist, to be with her. Although parts of you will complain, there is a deep 'Yes'. It will grow you. Even though the process is uncomfortable for her, it grows her and a new flower of life comes through you and her. What is unveiled in a relationship that is centred in truth, regardless of any pain known, is the development of deeper consciousness and deeper embodiment.

65

When A Man Moves With Clarity, He Is Love

"When there is real clarity, you are knowing as the pure Masculine Principle."

Q: I had an experience of such clarity of Knowing. Everything was so clear but now it is just a memory. What happened?

B: It is because when you had clarity you were a visitor. Man can be a tourist to clarity, particularly when he is around woman. He goes towards woman and is clear in the moment what the relationship is about, but because woman moves him to test his clarity he becomes unclear. She tests his depth and his belonging to clarity.

In some way, she has a deep knowing that to be one with him is to live the clarity that he is. She wants to feel the clarity deep in her body. She can move with that but she cannot move with a man who is unclear. If she does, she is less of a woman belonging to the principle of who She is. She is being her own victim of her own self.

To not be a visitor to clarity, you must move in the clarity. Moving in it will cost you all your likes and dislikes. Woman loves clarity, clarity given to her from a man who is the living clarity in the moment and it has his body and his heart. He to her is death or love, dependent on what she is willing to give away. If she is willing to give away, she will experience death and love immediately and she will experience the freshness of being with a clear man. She is not made 'other' in that moment, he is instantly what she is. She is not knowing two, there is no he or she. There is only One.

Q: Do you mean love, in terms of moving with the clarity?

B: That's right. When a man moves with clarity, he moves as love. If he does not move as clarity, he is not love. This affects the movement of his and the woman's forms that he is moving to. When he is clear and he is moving as clarity, she loves and knows his clarity. It is felt and known in her own body because she loves who he is. She instantly turns into his immediate love and he turns into her immediate love. They do not know two in that moment, they know one. She is willing to move to where he is willing to go, he is willing to go to where she is willing to move to. There is open space, both in the forms and in consciousness. There is a marriage happening.

Real love always costs you your old identities, old forms and old relationships. We are not talking about people in relationships. We are talking about how you relate to thoughts, feelings, conditions, forms. Forms are in every cell of your body. When you realise, your body shines and your form is light. When you live that kind of shining realisation, it changes the forms in your cells. As the forms in your cells change, the electromagnetic forces in your heart change the forms you relate to and a whole new life begins. You cannot pretend these things, they either are immediate and direct or you are moving your self to get tastes of this.

When there is clarity, you are knowing as the pure Masculine Principle. Sensation, the tingling that comes up, is pure sexual energy. Sensation is the deeper body of She coming up to turn that into form. Sensation is the embodiment of that clarity because true clarity is well beyond the body-mind identity. It is He or Him or the 'I' that I Am.

Often we have clarity as man and woman and then we have a sensation. When we move with both the clarity and the sensation we embody what we realised. Both principles came together to come into form because form is Consciousness, light, energy. It is pure.

66

True Naked Aware Awakening

"We are looking at man and woman from the perspective of the innermost and outermost, from the perspective of "I love woman as God" and "I love man as God." That perspective gives us an entrance into cosmic potentiality. Each and every moment begins to be a cosmic possibility."

Q: As we come to be living more and more from Being, deeper and deeper as man or woman, we become more capable to meet others from that deeper place. There can be beautiful energies exchanging regardless of gender, but in a deeper meeting between man and woman there is the possibility for that to move into a physical expression: lovemaking.

A woman might recognise the divinity in each man who is opening to that and a man might recognise that beautiful energy in each woman who is open to that, so it opens the possibility of multiple partners. My question is, how is that balanced with the heart, the necessity to go deeper and committed with one person? How do we balance that? How to navigate that?

B: First, let go of any conceptual idea that there is such a thing as man and woman. Let it go. Is there consciousness? Why divide? Go there first, you who is aware as Knowing. Awareness is knowing, if we look, not as man and woman, not as human, not as this, that or the other, but just look, we see that Awareness knows it knows. Explore that,

Awareness-Knowing is infinite.

As Awareness knows it is knowing the Self, for that is all that can be known, Pure Self. Awareness is knowing it knows. This is the Self knowing itself.

Start there, in the ground as Awareness-Knowing in which the cosmos arrives, universes arrive, forms arrive. You will then realise that as you stay true as Awareness to Knowing, you will know when you are moved on the level of man. You will be knowing as Awareness-Knowing, not as man, whether that movement comes from the unconditional nature of Knowing that knows it knows or whether that movement comes from a conditional aspect of self or person, through identification with past experience or wants and needs.

When you really get that clear, and I could speak to woman in very much the same way, then 'man and woman' is not dependent on 'man and woman'. Man and woman is dependent on Awareness knowing it knows.

Now this is the basis for a movement of relationship that is beyond the familiar sense of self but it is likely to come with the conditional sense of self. Unmix your knowing from sense objects or from the need to have woman, the need to have man by belonging purely to what you are knowing in the depth of your heart and beyond. It is quite rare to live in such a way but it is possible.

What is moving you then is so much more than any man or any woman. Your function as man of Consciousness is to *be* pure Knowing, fully open as Awareness. When that is also the function of woman, then there is a movement of

Masculine and Feminine power that is undivided. Within that movement as it comes into the body and into the experience of man and woman, there will be the emptying out of the belief of what a man should be, what a woman should be. It will all start to spill out.

You then discover what this calling or this pull to be together is. Is it a calling of want and need? Is it coming from a conditional sense of self? The psyche of humanity is still predominantly working from a conditional sense and you will come upon those conditions and your own conditions in these. Within that, you will find that woman will bring you all that you are to *be in* and not turn away.

When I say 'you', I am speaking of that that is *aware*, consciously aware appearing as man. It is a level. Keep going deeper and there is no man. You might come to the Principle of the Masculine but then that moves into the Self. So as a man growing in more openness of Awareness and being true to Knowing, you no longer move away from Knowing because of a need to protect any level of self on a mental, emotional or physical level.

You might begin to notice that woman will go straight to your weakness as Consciousness. She doesn't know she is doing this but she goes straight to that part of you for you to be opened and present in and to meditate the experience she has given you inside your heart and with your entire body.

When you as an aware man, Awareness as man, can really stay open in all that she gives you then it is no longer about what you are getting as a man, it becomes a functionality of Self-realisation. The Feminine Principle is drawing you to

Self-realise that that you both pour out of as the same one. Within that and your availability to come into multiple levels of death, you are dying to the old man that your father's father's father passed on. You are being so open without any need to have a conditional sense of being with her. Only then are you able to realise what She is and what She is in Awareness-Knowing.

She unwittingly burns out within man the holding on to a sense structure of 'being a man' and not Consciousness. She will come right into a place that needs development in the body-mind and evolution in the consciousness. She is not doing it as a woman. In this, she is the agency for the deeper meeting of what the Masculine and Feminine Principle is. All this will be a movement that unveils the possibility of true meeting.

Q: For someone like myself who might be in some intermediate stage of moving as Consciousness and Awareness, moving in that Is-ness and moving as self, would you advise to be with one woman, even though I might feel attraction to different women?

B: When you say 'such as myself' I am not knowing a 'my self', I am only knowing You direct, Awareness-Knowing. I am not knowing a man, I am only knowing the meeting. For the meeting of what you are to come all the way down into the possibility of expression as beingness expressing as man in his unconditional nature, all you can follow is your knowing, but not as a separate sense of self.

All the barriers to that are only in your mind. Within your mind is society, within your mind is the world, within our

212

mind is all the conditionality that says it looks this way or that way. You must come into your own Self-mastery, your own Self-enlightenment and your own loving of the knowing of what woman is in you. That is the movement of your life. No one can actually answer this question for you.

Woman comes to turn you into the master she knows is love. She is pointing you back into what you are, not out into man and woman. Man and woman don't come from man and woman. They come from the very essence of Consciousness itself. In moving as a man and as a woman you are going around in circles but in moving as Awareness awakening to Knowing within the seeing of woman and the knowing of Her, the seeing of man and the knowing of Him, the play is set for self-emptying but also for Self-enlightenment. Now you are in the possibility of truly meeting where she is utterly love, prior to where she was given a label as woman. This can be said to be the Feminine Principle. The Feminine Principle and the Masculine Principle are already one in the Self. Are they not seeking the other constantly to discover union in all things? Not just in man and woman but in all things.

When you get really clear to not move the old ways, no doubt you will see that you have old ways. Your question points to the true way and the way of an enlightened relating, knowing, meeting and being together.

I won't be giving you a formula for that, go this way or that way. You must discover it yourself. I suggest you only move by your deepest calling. There is no need in it but that that is profoundly true calls you to come into that meeting.

Discover in the meeting what it is that you are coming into. It is going to cost you your old way, your habits and your sense of self. It will cost you every bit of it and you will be tested along the way so you can see and know your self and move in the greater stream of what it is to be called to woman. In that, so much more than the man will be moving, so much more.

What will come up from the deep is more of what you are that you have not yet known, that you have to yet come into. Whatever she does, however she moves towards you is only about that, calling you to come deeper into what you really are without beginning and end and to find her in what She really is.

Any way your heart leads you to that, and it truly is your heart, then go that way. Other than that, I won't give you a formula. It will weaken you. You don't need strength to do this, you only need your heart's honesty to Knowing. No one else can show you the way. No one. Only you can discover it.

I can say to you that it is possible to realise the one light and the one Knowing in all of this. It will be the end of your limited sense of self and the alignment of all that you have on the surface, body, mind and intelligence with the deeper calling that moves the universe, dissolves it and remakes it. Within such a deep meeting it is not just you and woman who are changed but the entire universe, because you are the one that is moving the universe, You, Awareness-Knowing.

The ground of all this seeming surface experience is a clear experience, 'I am aware and knowing. I know.' Follow the light of Knowing. It is not knowing things, not even knowing woman. Follow Knowing knowingly as you truly see woman into what She is. This will have you revealing Her through You and She will reveal You through Her because You are both the same one. You have to stand alone in this. That is where your love lies, waiting.

This will open what you *are* together to what you are coming into. It is never about the persons, the selves, it is always about the Essence knowing and realising what it is amongst its forms of expression; greater union, deeper meaning having real form with no space or time in it. You will be unfolding the mystery of why you are called to even look at each other. What will begin to move is so much more than man and woman and you will be called to *be* that.

Realise and die cleanly within this, totally absorbed in the realising of the Knowing and the inner marriage consuming the calling to be together. This is what you will be coming to. This is very rare on the planet.

Most men and women are together to get something on the surface and keep everything comfortable. This will shatter every dream you ever had about what you are and what she is and yet true wonderment can move without being owned by a man and woman as 'someones'.

Q: I would have to include my whole body...

B: Let's get clear on what your whole body is, everything that you own, everything that you have in your life that you call mine is going to become divine, no longer yours. Everything. How you live, how you move, what you say, what you do, every level, every thought and feeling will be claimed. Every possession will be claimed. Every comfort will be claimed. Everything that you ever thought was yours will be claimed. Everything. Until there is nothing left but what you are together. The rarest realisation on the planet.

Look how man and woman struggle with that: "Me, me, mine, mine!" She has come to take everything of form away from you, so that you really get that you *are* the formless nature of Consciousness and She *is* the movement of the light of love dancing with your formlessness, yet you are the same one.

In this union there is nothing that you are going to own, not even Monday, Tuesday, Saturday or Sunday, not day, not night, not anything. This is how good it gets. True naked aware awakening into what the principles in the light of love and in the beingness of truth are, without beginning and end. There is no return ticket.

You cannot have her for yourself. She cannot have you for her self. It is all for God or the realisation of Self and its movement throughout all existence. I can see how much you love that. I see it, there is a love of the essence of Knowing. But if you take one look towards identification with the name you give yourself or with where you believe you live, you go to lesser Self-realisation in the call to meet woman, or for woman to meet man in the essence of Pure Consciousness and the movement that moves the universe as that meeting.

Any thought of 'me' and you have gone to sleep, any thought of 'other' and you have gone to sleep. Any thought of 'this is too much' or 'I can go', you have gone to sleep. I presume you want the highest teaching. Here it is.

You will know when you become mobile as a 'someone' in that calling, when you are not on a unicycle but on your bicycle, duality. Uni is one, belong to that alone and there is no turning any other way. In this, the deep opens. It is very rare, the realisation of the essence of God or pure Awareness, knowing itself.

You will love forgetting yourself. She will definitely help you lose your mind and you will definitely help her find her heart and it is the mind of God and the heart of God because that is all there is.

Interview On True Tantra

"True tantra is the giving up of oneself. I am speaking of a higher purpose where the love, the calling is completely and utterly to dissolve egoic distractions both in the man and the woman, to bring about the pure living of love on earth and the pure demonstration of what truth is.

Man and woman are bringing in the frequencies of deeper higher resonances into all their activities. This is definitely going to burn out the ego and each are going to face themselves in the fire of that love.

Mainstream tantra focuses on orgasm, sex energy and eroticism, having a good time for the 'me'. This is still conditionality in that the calling is to bring each other to truth. We are already one because in existence truth is love, and love is truth."

67

Authentic Attraction IS Authentic Tantra

Interview by Cynthia Connop – Australia

"Tantra is a way to Self-realisation. It is the embodiment of Self-realisation as one body of the Masculine and Feminine."

Q: How does your teaching differ from mainstream tantra?

B: First we have to define what we see as mainstream tantra. What I see on websites and in holistic or New Age magazines around the world, is that tantra is solely about sex and orgasm, about excitement and getting something for yourself, for the 'me'. This is particularly so on websites where images of scantily clad women portrayed as goddesses are the norm.

What I do not see in mainstream tantra is the word love or truth. That is true tantra, the unifying of all opposites through sense perception, through expression in this body in pure sexuality. This connection has to be from deep within the heart, whereas mainstream tantra is about enjoying something for the self. To me, tantra is the giving up of one's self. It is the deepening embodiment of love between two people who truly love the divine and whose whole life is about truth. If their whole life is about truth, what they are seeing in their connection together is the oneness behind the forms of the Masculine and the Feminine and yet those forms are dancing as the Masculine and Feminine. That is the calling, giving themselves only to truth. Nothing else is going to burn out all their egoic ways. They are going to have to penetrate the illusion of sexing each other, particularly the male sex-oriented way of *having* woman.

True tantra is not about sexual excitement. It is about entering the stillness together and the pleasure that is encountered in going into that profundity of stillness, opening these bodies, which is beyond what I have heard of in mainstream tantra. I am speaking of the full transformation of the Masculine and the Feminine in intimate union. That means great honesty and great integrity, with nothing left for the 'me' to hold onto. It means seeing through the veil of illusion that love is about 'me' getting anything and having the courage, the power and wisdom to penetrate that with more intimate connection. Through the making of love, through intimacy to one's self and with the other, making a deeper and deeper connection, you come up against so much past and so much distraction, you have to divine your way through it. That means there must be a real purpose for this connection and it does not involve the 'me'. It is the dissolution of the 'me'.

Q: Yes, that's one path of mainstream tantra but there is the other aspect of it. Here people aim to use the energy that would normally go into procreation for spiritual transformation.

B: That is exactly what I'm saying - we are Being, or the One Self appearing as gender or principles. The attraction is that we sit in two different polarities, two completely different functions, and the draw is to bring those two polarities together in oneness. I am speaking of the energy of the love that is being used or directed to deeper or higher states of love, deeper or higher states of pure Knowingness that transcend egoity, to bring man into true polarity and to bring woman into true polarity, to bring each other into truth where there is no polarity. That is the direct communication of love, the direct realisation of truth beyond gender.

I am speaking of a higher purpose where the love, the attraction is used completely and utterly to dissolve egoic distractions both in man and woman, to bring about the pure living of love on earth and the pure demonstration of what truth is. Therefore, you are bringing in the frequencies of deeper or higher resonances in your activities. That will burn out the ego and man and woman will face themselves in the fire of that love.

Mainstream tantra focuses on orgasm, sex energy and eroticism, on having a good time for a 'me',which is still conditionality. True tantra is to bring each other to truth because instantly in existence, truth is love and love is truth. You have unified all opposites and you live with your partner and all beings as that ecstatic state of aliveness, yet in the deepest place the background of your life is totally at peace.

Harmony just happens. It is not actually about orgasm, the woman striving for an orgasm or the man striving for an orgasm because that is still pulling up something for an individual egoic self, somebody who still needs something. If orgasm happens that is fine, but really it is about truth. That is the true making of love, where love opens and flows through both the Masculine and Feminine Principles into truth, into love, into Pure Being, pure openness. I am speaking about life man and woman, its total direction being the expression of love and the deepest truth. What comes from this are states of stillness beyond Knowing, states of nothingness beyond even gender that burst open as the Shakti that opens into straightness as the pure Masculine, and opens up into orgasmic pleasure for both the man and woman. Opening into ecstatic states is secondary to the knowing of nothingness as the Source, the knowing of truth as the Source. Then all activity flows out of that unnameable place of peace and flows into pure creativity, joy and bliss.

What I pick up from my journeys around the world is that most of tantra is for what you can get out of it for your own orgasmic pleasure. I am speaking about the embodiment of love, which is grounded in stillness. When we as man and woman put stillness first, which is honesty and truth, then the bodies open from a heart-centred place.

Q: There is a huge divorce rate now, relationships are failing and people don't really know what to do, so how can what you are offering help the ordinary couple? How do they reach this state you speak of? What can they actually do?

B: First, you have to come to the truth that sex without love is a distortion, that true sexuality is the living for truth and that is the unfolding in existence of love. Without love, without truth, without deep honesty, sex is the pain and disturbance that we see as the whole world, the egoic attraction of getting what you want and never being fulfilled. It does not quench your thirst. True love, which is the death of the 'me' or the transformation of the 'me', quenches your thirst in the knowledge of who You are.

Woman is the embodiment of love and she has to learn to not step out of that by going up into her head. Man, he is the embodiment of truth and he has to learn to not step out of that for his own egoity, for his own material, mental and emotional gains. There has to be some real purpose in this draw to be together.

Is this attraction much more than these two bodies? The bodies are part of the attraction as we are learning how to love through existence to that non-existent state. But that non-existent place is also love here as existence. That is the ending of polarity and the knowing and living of union. That is the true endeavour between man and woman.

Your love has to have a higher or deeper purpose and that means greater honesty within your own heart to what is true in each and every moment, beyond past and future. We learn to navigate through life's various obstacles of egoity, for instance, the coming up of past patterns, to embrace each other in what is and not in what could be, should be or what was. We are showing each other a way of love that is eternal because it is always here and nowhere else. That is the purging of any movement in space and time to get anything different than what is Here.

Q: What would be an example of that? Say you are a couple and you have kids and are busy. What can this couple do? How can they apply what you are talking about?

B: This takes an awful lot of power. It is the power of seeing the truth in all things, the love of seeing the truth in all things whereby you begin to discover your deepest knowing is what is true. That is what you have to function from. Your life in each moment must fit your deepest knowingness. Of course, as we face ourselves in the mirror of this love, initially 'stuff' can be flying all over the place. Any reaction to that is not in our deepest knowing but that reaction becomes our teacher as we call each other to be more authentic. If we do not let that 'stuff' go from what our honesty reveals, it is always going to disturb us individually on the surface. Then we are never going to get into this love of our being together because we are always being pulled back up to re-address the surface.

We are together to dive into the deep. Only this brings a calm joy of pure potentiality up to our manifest surface life. Through your deepest knowing together, life begins to give you a way or a passage through. You stay in the present and your life becomes more balanced because you are giving up your pressure of living for the truth of love. You are learning to rest in your knowingness each and every moment. It is that knowingness or intelligence that begins to move life in a way of harmony. This does not take five minutes, it is going to take your entire presence. Then harmony will just deepen and deepen. Most people start with setting aside a time to be more intimate and it can be heartfelt, but I guarantee that intimate heartfelt time is going to bring up your past. It is going to hit the fan because that is its job, love's job is to purify the energy of the distracted self into wholeness.

You cannot have love without this arising of the past. It is almost impossible because you are inviting your past to come home to the present. Do you have the willingness to stop for a moment, see it as the past, and continue to embrace each other in love until that passes through? By getting on with the loving and not allowing what arises to disturb you but to see through it? In that, you are not constantly throwing the past onto each other but divining your way through it in the present, by your knowing of what you are doing together. Look at any arising of the past from a place of pure intelligence. That is pure love.

From that, you literally begin to undo the past by the love of the moment. You begin to speed up your consciousness. Eventually as that happens, the past is no longer a problem because you are in a place unaffected by it. You are the power of love itself. It is about transformation.

Transformation is when you begin to live together in the love of the moment and serve the truth behind all this. It comes in stages as you grasp the idea, the essential idea that woman is pure love. She is endeavouring to experience her love directly and man is endeavouring to mirror to her that she is the embodiment of pure love. That means that neither of them must get familiar. They must remain as though they have just met, as much as possible.

Obviously, there are the ordinary things of life, such as bill paying and the daily chores that get taken care of naturally, because life has integrity in all things. At the same time, connecting with each other in a deep respectful way as Being, as the profundity of love, is taking responsibility for your self, the small self, the 'me'. Woman takes responsibility for that and man takes responsibility for that. You are not healing each other. You are basically being true to your innermost being. He is reflecting the awesome love that She is and woman is reflecting the awesome truth that He is, through the love in which she is being held. This is not something that you work on. This is you dissolving in and cutting into the deepest place in yourself through the integrity of what has pulled you together.

The old way would be to make your pain better by having sex or creating some other distraction. This will last five minutes or however long it does and creates an energy that is going to hit you both in the face again, whereas the making of love, or being as love from the purest place, fuels the transformation and opens the divinity of the bodies directly and profoundly. There has to be a 'seeing' that you are the temples of the divine, but truly see it. You cease being familiar with each other or with yourself. You are inspiring each other to be alive and true.

Q: The other thing that I have noticed a lot in mainstream tantra is ejaculation control and semen retention particularly in the Taoist approach. Do you see a role for that in your way of lovemaking?

B: As I said before the making of love is not about reaching orgasm either for male or for the female. It is about entering into and the embodiment of more love. Retention of semen is not something that is needed, other than for the loving to go deeper. For me there is a natural place for orgasm to take place. Sometimes it might not even take place for the man or for the woman.

He has to control his ejaculation because he has built up so much excitement through his sexual neediness of woman, and projected so much onto her. It is all energy in his body, in his mind, particularly stuck down in his genitals. When he comes to meet her, all that excitement comes out as premature ejaculation or as 'sexuality projected onto her'. He is projecting his sex onto her and not serving her as love.

There is also the past pain and emotion woman is holding in her body. Man has to have the capacity to hold her in greater stillness, to be able to take through his body her surrender. If he is not deep enough in his body, in his life, the release of her energy can cause him to ejaculate. At first, he might need to learn a technique but what truly does this, is profound love. True devotion to the Feminine, the mirror of his innermost love, and true honesty takes him way beyond ejaculation because it changes a part of the brain that is connected to the genital area. When he is really in devotion to her with no projection, the power of his innermost presence comes to the fore of his consciousness and he is now in expression as his love for her.

His practice in every moment of his life is non-projection because it is that projection that causes him to get excited, causes him to get sexual, and causes him to project onto life. That projection is the egoity or the 'me'. It triggers off more excitement and he ejaculates or becomes a sexual monster. He is just using woman. I would say that most women would recognise that energy in man.

Man's practice to go beyond ejaculation is an everyday practice of not being in projection but serving love, serving truth. Now comes the paradox. When he is not in projection, he is true projection because he is the positive force of the One appearing as man, as she is the negative force, or openness, of the One appearing as woman. I say 'appearing' because they are to me the One Self in movement and polarity, the One Self moving as the Feminine and Masculine.

The whole body of woman is in the same pure frequency as the vagina. Likewise, the whole body of the man is in the same pure frequency as the phallus and that is the polarity at play as these bodies. The phallus functions within its own intelligence from the heart coupled with a deep connection from pure Mind. It is not after orgasm, it is not after getting anything from a woman. The phallus is a devotional instrument of the divine to the Feminine, keeping her existent self opened into the truth and flow of eternal love, for that is what She truly is.

When a man finds deeper purpose in his life and in his attraction to woman, the phallus becomes pure intelligence functioning from the heart. In lovemaking the phallus seeks the vagina from its own intelligence. It is pretty awesome for a man who has never experienced the phallus being in intelligence, as if it has its own eyes and its own knowing, and it can literally find the vagina energetically and the vagina recognises the Pure Consciousness of the phallus. The woman experiences the vagina suddenly becoming its own intelligence and opening up to receive the principle of the phallus all on its own. The consciousness of the male and the female is left in awe watching these two principles at play, love play.

The attraction is very pure and yet it happens in such a completely authentic and original way that the consciousness of man and woman that was stuck in mind and in the 'me' orientation, has the opportunity to wake up to their divine pure essence. This is within the vagina and phallus, inclusive of the whole body and yet beyond it because that is what the bodies really are, the manifest consciousness of Masculine and Feminine polarities, of which the genitals are the manifest doorways to these profound expressions of the One.

For a man and woman to have that experience is a pretty extraordinary awakening into what man and woman really is. For Consciousness to be fully awake beyond the body is awesome. That does not happen when you are looking for something from the woman through excitement, when the man is exciting the woman. He has to be completely and utterly devotional to her divine essence in a way of truth, where he is holding her in such stillness that he is also calling her to be authentic and surrender herself, not to surrender to him but to the powers that are beckoning them both to come into what love really is. Now that is a rare state of tantra.

Q: What do you mean when you say man is projection?

B: You only have to look at the shape of the bodies, which are manifest mirrors of the particular polarities, to see that man is the projective or positive half and woman is the negative, pure, opened half. He projects.

Man is pretty lost if he does not have a project. He is lost if he does not have a purpose, or a vision. His deepest vision is the vision of wholeness, of pure creativity. This involves feminine energy because it is the feminine energy that creates. He is the principle of divine purpose or pure idea. Woman has the masculine in her as well, but he is the embodiment of that, whereas she is the embodiment of creativity in terms of feminine energy. He is the embodiment of the whole idea, a masculine energy within the whole of creation. So his job as the projection is in the service or the serving of that vision within the divine body of the Feminine appearing as existence.

He is the projection, and he says: "I have got this idea, I have got that idea". I am suggesting that if woman says that, it is her inner male energy. If he says: "This is tender, this is beautiful, this is so soft" - speaking in openness in that way - it is his Feminine speaking. So this whole mystery is the embodiment of the Masculine and the Feminine, living principles that are in both man and woman endeavouring to unify within themselves and as unified expressions as love in existence. For those two bodies to join together in their physical sensuality, in their true heartfelt purpose, the bodies open up all the way into the primary energy of the Masculine and the Feminine and go beyond that into the One Self.

Back to the projection, that is why he has the phallus. He projects as it were his divine purpose and yet she surrenders to hers. Hers is an opening; his is a projection.

Woman can feel man's projection when he is not in his true purpose. She feels his projection as a psychic disturbance, annoyance, or pain. That is when he is projecting his egoity, his 'me' purpose. When he is moving from profound truth in a way of love, she feels that as openness inside herself. She does not close to that. She closes to his projection but she opens to his living of truth.

Q: I would imagine that women who are listening are going 'Yes, great. How can I invite this from my man or how can I be with a man that is living this?' What would you say to women who are touched by what you are saying?

B: First, I must point towards the deepening of the Feminine and the deepening of the Masculine because on the surface nothing is at it seems. It seems man is man and woman is woman but both the Masculine and the Feminine Principles are so deep, it depends on whether the man or the woman is functioning out of shallowness, from their conditioning. The invitation in this loving is to draw each other back to the very root of the Feminine and the Masculine.

A woman in the beginning may make a problem of 'You are closing me down, but yesterday you were opening me up'. That is a stage woman has to go through until she begins to trust that she is the embodiment of love. She has the reflection of it as the earth, the knowing of it as herself, if she descends deep enough. As she ceases projection, a male trait, projecting out, she begins to come down into where love really resides, in the heart, and she recognises that is what she is. In this relatedness as the love of truth, they are inviting each other to go beyond their conditionality into deeper and deeper places, towards the very core of what they are, being Feminine and being Masculine, being One Self.

Let's say a woman is living this embodiment of love. She has probably gone through hell with the man in her life and she is ceasing projecting love 'out there' like her mother's mother did and her sisters. She has been bringing herself back into the knowing of love within and encountering more of what she is as the Feminine. That will draw a deeper man who is not projecting that love is outside himself, in a woman's body, but sees the mirror of his innermost love as the embodiment of woman. He gets to see the mirror of that in existence from a deeper purer way. That is what woman is really drawn to in her attraction to man. A woman with a deepening experience of her divine place as the pure Feminine will know when a man is in projection and it will not bother her. She will not close - because she has opened beyond herself, beyond her fears and doubts.

Q: What do you mean when you say man is in projection?

B: What I mean by this is that man represents stillness or non-movement in his deepest place. We could call it presence. He does not have any agendas. He does not have anything to do in this place. He is that that is in total observation of life as it is. This is at his root where there is no activity, and should a woman move into his presence, her experience of his non-activity would be to come into full openness, full flowering. Her radiant beauty would shine utterly. This is the truth of what takes place within the emptiness of the Masculine when met by the innocence of the Feminine. Between the two, pure creativity happens.

When a man has movement of mind, a projection of his linear identity as a 'someone', his presence lacks the purity of being no-one. He is literally seeking, through mind, something to do, any distraction, particularly sexual that will ease his pain of not being himself, still, silent and present. Of course, in what I am speaking of here, the man has to have reached a certain level of spiritual maturity for him not to be distracted in life and to come to understanding that to use his power to project as 'want' or 'need' onto woman, onto life, is unreal, is egoic.

When a man is in true polarity, he is utterly still and present. When life moves him to create, his movement would be in service to love and to truth where there is nothing to gain but the sheer pleasure of being himself. Then he is also no longer disturbed by experiencing that woman is emotional. He can love from a deeper place. He has the capacity to embrace that emotion much more because he is a deeper man. That is the calling for both man and woman, to attract each other into deeper and deeper places of being Masculine, being Feminine, being the One.

Q: Because we are talking about tantra, and we touched on it earlier about using the procreation energy, taking it up through the chakras and into higher Consciousness, into enlightenment...

B: I have never practiced any of that in my entire life. Yet without practicing that, it became my direct experience. It just came upon me, not once but several times throughout my life, until it became my utter state of love. I have experienced the full embodiment of the Masculine and the Feminine, the full enlightenment of my being and the full enlightenment of the Feminine within myself. I experienced that without any practicing of bringing energy up the body. All I have ever been in my life is in devotion to truth and to love, although I would not have used those words a few years ago, it was just my nature, and everyone's sweetest nature is that.

Our sweetest nature is that we love. It does not matter that it is covered over with our conditioning. This man experienced that with the Feminine, experienced that as man, experienced that as oneness, without any practices other than the pure attraction to the Feminine, the pure attraction to life and the pure deep attraction to that unspeakable place. It came about just because I love.

You can see how I am on fire with that because it is so simple. It really is so simple. I did not practice breathing or anything else. It just all took place because I love, and that is what I am suggesting that people do, intelligently in each moment, look to the deeper place in their activity, look to the deeper place within their attraction and give their life to that. That is what opens up and unifies all the chakras. Truth does it all, truth in existence being love. It is in the integrity, the simple honesty to your deepest knowing that it just happens.

Q: Are you saying that people can go directly to the Source, and start from there rather than try and do practices to get there?

B: To me there is nothing to practice because we *are* that. But then there are the layers and layers of conditioning. Radical simple honesty to what truth reveals in each moment opens your limited perspective, your trapped consciousness in body-mind identity, to the unlimited expression or potentiality of that that You truly are. It opens, in the simplicity of what life already is. There is no need to make a Hollywood movie of all this. It is already what we are. We can unfold it in the simplicity of life but that takes direct honesty. Honesty reveals what love and truth really is. In that, energies naturally ascend, descend, and display themselves.

I can give you a very simple event in my life. There have been many like this. There was a woman in England who used to ask me to come and give seminars to her friends. There was great friendship there, but no intimacy. We were just about to say goodbye, to give each other a hug and immediately with no warning I was completely and utterly in my energetic presence as Masculine, directly. I was no longer the body-mind identity, the physical. And this was her experience too, neither was she. Suddenly we were in this entwining energy that was just incredible, an entwining flowing flame. This is the holy flame. There was this trinity of divinity happening. It was so beautiful and so beyond this body-mind identity. Then we became aware of the senses. We stood gazing at each other but from another place entirely, not from the perspective of body-mind but completely and absolutely from the pure Masculine and the pure Feminine essence. Then we began to laugh and laugh and laugh, so beautiful, tears streaming down our face at that beautiful and uncalled for union. That is the kind of experience with the Feminine I have had throughout my life.

Q: It is interesting that you were talking about the divine because possibly what people are searching for with tantra is to bring the sacred into their life and into their relationships and lovemaking. Do you have anything that you would like to say about that?

B: Let's speak about nurturing, nurturing without neediness. Nurturing without neediness is to know deep within the heart that there is so much more here in this attraction of the

Masculine and the Feminine than the conditions that we know and experience. We begin to nurture that knowing and that knowing begins to move our bodies or inform us of our actions in embracing this knowingness, and giving it form. The nurturing is that you are listening so deep to the heart space and it is the heart space that informs the mind of what to do, what to let go of and how to be. You follow that.

For instance you are in your bedroom and normally you might jump in, turn over and go to sleep, or you might just have sex together, the normal thing of just fulfilling each other but not in You. We have no need to do that. Your knowing might say, now hold a moment, just stop, and look into each other's eyes, hold hands, just gently breathe and keep dropping your mind's idea of what this is, who you are and who she is, who you are and who he is.

Keep dropping your ideas and your conditions away. Let nothing be there but this female body, this male body, this room and whatever this is. Let it all keep dropping away. Then something might happen where a greater tenderness and a greater stillness comes through the body. You are listening to the deepest place and giving it action or form. That listening requires greater and greater awareness of the intention within oneself. You are not getting busy and being directed by your mind and what you should do or should not do. You are listening from a deeper place that animates this body. That is the Pure Consciousness of the Feminine and the Masculine.

You are listening and a greater stillness is coming up, a greater nothingness is coming up and that is the space in which love is really made. Where the new begins to animate the bodies; new consciousness as the Masculine and new consciousness as the Feminine. It is a different way of being together because you are listening to something that has not been here before. You are not listening to your mind saying you have done this before or you should do this. You are nurturing the peace within the silence and functioning from that place.

Q: So you wouldn't know what's going to happen or what it is going to look like. Is that right?

B: That is right. That is the very nature of realised Consciousness, anything that is known is but a reflection of the past. The real is experienced Now, eternal expression that is here in each moment expressing the new. There is no time in the eternal expression, only in the human mind. The human mind has to be emptied as the eternal mind, and then Being human becomes an eternal experience where everything is new consciousness expressed as love.

It is our mind that delineates it and that is the cause of all our suffering. We can open our minds by opening our hearts to see that all that is here is the eternal expression of oneness appearing here as man and woman.

Q: Does devotion play a part in sacred intimacy?

B: We are devoted to truth, devoted to love, and then that devotion becomes particular to that woman, to that man, but it has no 'particular' in it and that is the paradox. You have to see beyond the man and woman.

Q: How does woman serve man?

B: Woman serves man in her devotion to truth. She has to have a greater love for truth than she does for the man, otherwise she will confuse the man with 'her truth' or 'her love'. When she serves truth she knows what is true from deep inside her own real experience. I am not talking about 'She' in terms of the individual egoic woman; I am talking about the divine principle coming through that woman. She serves the man by having a greater love for truth than the man because that attraction then heightens or calls a man to be truer than he has ever been prior to this moment.

When a man is really living out of the truth of his own being, she recognises that as the truth she loves, and she instantly loves the man. There is complete alignment with the truth. In that moment, he is living truth, he is eternal and that is what she loves. Unless she loves truth more than she loves anything else, she is not calling the man to live authentically from the deep well of his own being. She is calling him to be authentic, to be original, to not live from past patterning. She says: "Go beyond your name, go beyond your identity, and be formlessly alive in this form. What is the truth of this moment? Die for it!" That is what she is asking of him.

She is the deep, the Feminine Principle that is calling him. She yearns to meet 'He', the pure Masculine, the Lord of the universe, in this ordinary expression of man. They are wooing each other up, the pure Masculine, the pure Feminine, in the bodies of man and woman. They meet in the form, authentic bodies as themselves.

She serves him by giving him the opportunity to be in his deepest truth and living it. That is how she serves him and that is how she serves the Feminine too, because the Feminine is calling for authentic love in the man. She is loving the man to be completely and absolutely original, no past, no future, only the real Here. If there is any other consideration, then she is not being the pure Feminine.

Q: What is the deepest purpose of this teaching? What is the ideal vision of living this way?

B: The deepest purpose obviously is not just about man and woman. They are universal expressions within existence and yet beyond existence. The deepest purpose is absolute realisation as the Feminine or the Masculine. When the Feminine or the Masculine reach the realisation of the Absolute, there is neither Feminine nor Masculine. The funny thing is, in my experience that brings the authentic consciousness of the Masculine and Feminine truly alive. If you see that from the place of original time or timelessness, where sense perception is at its cleanest, prior to the egoic mind coming in, what keeps the bodies of the Feminine and Masculine pure is the love of the Absolute, the Source from which they come.

When they love that un-nameable place more than each other because each other comes from the authentic absolute place, instantly a woman is pure Feminine and instantly a man is pure Masculine. As we bring honesty into our relationships and into ourselves, there is the potential that we truly are being in the full dance of this life.

Q: We have the idea of monks on a celibate spiritual path…

B: How could he arrive on the earth without woman? How can he be embodied here without woman? For me it is quite clear that the purpose in this domain of expression is the cosmic play, where that mystery of the Self has seemingly split itself into two without going into duality. Most teachings think that this is duality. It is not duality. It is the One playing the game of the two.

When man and woman are in their authentic essence, although she is completely and absolutely Feminine and he is completely and absolutely Masculine, in their union they are completely and utterly nothing, because they are the play of truth. When we step into that place in the moment there is the potential for that energy to wipe out all the patterning in our subconscious and for us not to be a puppet of that patterning. That means you must have a greater purpose in your life. Otherwise you will not be able to face the seeming onslaught of a death of what you thought you were as the 'me'. You will not be able to face it, it will be like you are dying. You will not be able to transform your life as a vibrant expression of what already is out there as the trees, the ocean and the whole of nature.

Q: How would the world look if your form of tantra were really embodied in couples?

B: It would not be different, it would be authentic, but it would be non-difference. Non-difference is: everything would be returned to 'as it is'. All the rest of the stuff is illusion, a projection of mind-orientated creativity. When we let go of the projection of the 'me', we simply return to that authentic place and realise that that is all there is. I can say in authentic realisation that everything is seen to be complete.

Everything is seen to be an expression as the One because it is. It is not seen as duality.

I see that it is, it is my direct experience - I am the One. Leaves, birds, plants, sky, man, woman, everything is oneness. Everything already is this, because this is the eternal reflection where everything is renewed. Renewal is the only constant in the universe of form. The consciousness behind all this is renewing the form instantly from a place of authenticity. It is the mind that clouds this already perceived state of purity, begins to look through past therefore creating a future and therefore clouds of illusion. These clouds of illusion have created the sub-conscious that divides us from the direct experience of the pure human psyche that is one with Source, the subconscious being the storehouse of all our past and future expectations, all the pain of rejection and un-fulfillment. Yet there is nothing wrong in that because it can bring about radical transformation, through burning enough fire in your living of truth through your experience of life until it dawns on your mind and opens in your heart that you are already That.

You are already free. All that I am saying is that the attraction to gender and the making of love are the very expressions or components of unified existence. It already is taking place but when the intelligence of man and woman join together from conditionality they create greater and greater illusion and store up more conditioned energy, the subconscious. Unconditional energy is universal love or intelligence. We can be opened by that in any moment, whether it is through tantra or some other teaching. Because all teachings really, and that is inclusive of tantra, are not about getting a better life in the future. They are about learning to be fully present, fully aware, fully true, fully embodied in a way of love Now. It is the discovery that this already is the truth, you are not heading towards this, it already IS this. Hence, the shedding of all the shadows that you have been looking through. The biggest shadows are through the attraction of man and woman because for existence to even happen, there has to be attraction. For this beautiful experience to happen there has to be the Masculine and Feminine Principles and that dance of seemingly dualistic consciousness at play. In truth, it is no dance, it is the One as two and it is so beautiful.

What is not beautiful about it is the storehouse of personal consideration, and yet, this is all part and parcel of the game for Consciousness has created animal bodies, molded and refined them into the shapes of man and woman, so that love may meet love, truth may meet truth and Consciousness may know its Self beyond all expressions within expression. That is the cosmic game that we are all involved in so that we may know ourselves as the Source of all life, and beyond.

We, as human consciousness, are still in the process of entering the animal bodies intelligently. Through entering the body but not identifying with the body or the mind, we discover that we as man and woman are masters of the universe, or the masters of love coming into matter creating form and instantly dissolving into formless energy. We think we are not in command of all that but we are. We are what gives this form as principles, as divine beings.

About B

"When I say 'I', I am not speaking of someone called B Prior I am speaking as the only 'I' in the universe that is emptiness and yet full."

68

About B

Born in 1954 in England, B's childhood and teenage years were marked by profound mystical experiences. At age 19 he awakened in the realisation of oneness and at 33 he opened into the Absolute. Within this unfolding he was graced with the rare and profound realisation of the Bhagavati, the divine Feminine Principle. Following realisation his known life up to that point was entirely shattered. A life of service in utter dedication to the awakening and evolution of humanity began and continues to unfold.

B offers a profoundly unique and enlightening perspective on life from the smallest matters that shape our personal lives to the biggest universal questions of human existence. His teaching and transmission is the ultimate calling to awaken as Awareness-Knowing. With true compassion, humour and uncompromising truth, B brings the highest teaching straight to our core and into daily life. His call is to profoundly awaken whilst living in the world and his discourses cover all areas of life - relationships, sexuality, work and creativity, parenting and children, all brought to an awakening heart of Conscious Awareness.

B currently lives in New Zealand and travels extensively offering talks, seminars and residential retreats. People around the world come to B as they are waking up from the dream and conditional belief of a separate sensed self.

B is the Originator of The Form Reality Practice, a powerful movement practice and vehicle of awakening that is the living embodiment and transmission of realisation. He is the Founder of She Universe, a vibrant community in New Zealand dedicated to the awakening and living of one's highest possibility of love and creativity.

69

Beyond The Beyond

"A Master is a location of infinite Consciousness that is no-thing yet it is locatable. You dive into that Master and you are no longer going to be locatable."

I come to you as Awareness-Being. I don't see you sitting there in form. My name is B Prior. I Am prior to form, I Am where form springs from, even prior to Being. When I speak like this I am not speaking about 'someone' on the chair; that is a manifestation of what 'This' is. Those that come, I point in the same direction as the realisation here.

No one actually gets enlightened but there is a return of Awareness moving into Knowing, which is light, the Self. Enlightenment then is Awareness no longer getting confused with the sense of self as a 'me'.

***

I was with about twelve people over a seven day period on a retreat, the only retreat I have ever, ever been on, but realisations have been happening all my life. I was sitting on a chair and I completely went in, beyond the beyond the beyond. At first I was conscious, consciously going in and I realised the universe and then I realised this huge sound, which I knew to be my Self. It wasn't Bernie Prior knowing this, it was the knower of the universe knowing this.

If you know anything, it is the knower of the universe. You adapted to being something less than the knower of the universe. You believe you are the knower of your little life, but in truth you are the knower of the universe. The knower of the universe was knowing itself and its universe and its universal body. Then the knower of the universe was knowing all the elements and how it put everything together. All the elements appeared in Awareness as Consciousness.

Please keep forgetting Bernie Prior in this. I went in between and up the shaft of the elements and this huge sound began and I realised that sound was 'I'. It was my return, the sound of my coming home, but I also knew it to be the sound of Creation, all omnipresent in one instant. I disappeared and there was no knower, there was just pure Awareness. There was no knower. I can describe this now. I couldn't then.

Awareness became aware once again of the entire cosmos. Awareness became aware of streams of Beingness and then Awareness became aware of a body of earth. Then Awareness became aware of a body and then - this is not easy to explain, there was Awareness and Awareness had the Consciousness to see the entire room as its own bright radiant Awareness having its own bright Consciousness. Awareness was knowing Consciousness. Consciousness was knowing Awareness. It was all being known, everything was being known. It was all Now - absolutely clear, absolutely nothing but 'What Is'.

Then something shifted and when the shift occurred Awareness suddenly became aware of the body, then Awareness was Awareness having Consciousness in a body. There was still no Bernie Prior.

Awareness looked around the room at these other people who were looking a little amazed at what was going on in this Bernie Prior person on the chair. Awareness could see the universe of each and everyone but they were not bodies, they were universes. They were universes inside the universe and Awareness knew they weren't aware of this.

Awareness then became 'this man'. In that instant when Awareness became 'this man', something else took place. It was as though my head lifted off like a thousand petals and as Awareness, as Consciousness, as the Masculine, as this man, I entered the entire universe. It was the birth of God and it dropped right the way round my entire body. It was like an egg of vibrant radiant Awareness having Consciousness - Pure Being.

There was no way I could go back to the way I was. There was no way.

70

She Didn't Just Come Here, She Fully Embodies Me

"I have integrated the Masculine and Feminine as my own Real Self. 'He-She' or 'Shiva-Shakti' is That, that I Am."

Realisation opened up for me the truth that Pure Self expresses in Pure Consciousness and Pure Energy, which is the Feminine Principle. That marriage, of that that is already in union, gives birth to the cosmos and to every universe within the cosmos. The Bhagavati is the power and presence of love behind all forms. She is the movement of those forms and the relationship between them. She relates to profound Consciousness, the Masculine Principle. It became apparent that the love that I am as She comes into existence as the love of a woman and the love of a man in the nature of Godhood and in the nature of living realisation.

In my realisation of the Feminine Principle, She first came out of my heart and looked at me and I knew Her. Later She arrived in a human form. In the realisation of the Absolute I knew Her. I am speaking as Awareness because as I realised the profoundly deep, I realised that She is the expression, the display as the entire cosmos of the deep. She is the body of the deep. She is Now, coming up, radiating out. She has no beginning and no end as She gives form to the formless.

Most Buddha statues have many little swirls on the crown. That is Her display. She showed me that She is so much more than that. She is the entire manifestation of the cosmos. She did not just 'come here', She fully embodies me."

71

Tantric Master

"Being with a living Master opens you to walk the deeper pure realms of your own real being and to manifest these realms as your life leading to the realisation of your True Self."

A Tantric Master is a power that descends to earth taking on form to embody the figure eight of infinity; the holy marriage of form and formlessness. He is the ringing that calls both formlessness into form and form into formlessness. He is the door in which the holy marriage takes place, where 'everybody' returns to being 'nobody', pure Awareness Consciousness that instantly becomes embodied. This is the highest possibility in the presence of this power.

A living Tantric Master transmits this power through and as his body. He takes on the world in humanity and empties it out of its selfishness, its anguish, ignorance, doubts and fears, to be returned to innocence; the love of God. In this, he opens the earth to live its destiny to create God in form as man and woman. He transmits higher reality into their consciousness and into their bodies.

Man is returned to his nobility, his true authority, that that gives direction to all of life, his true power to bring the unseen into the seen. Woman is returned to her true state, which is love, the need to know no-thing. As a higher-level woman she weaves the formlessness of the deep into true form and true relationship with the most high.

I may be misunderstood where the expression of the essence of love and truth is translated into a language of self. I am not speaking of B Prior I am speaking of HIM who has been here many, many times, wearing different colored skin. I am HE and I am also HER. I am the divine Mother, I am the divine Father and I am also the blessed Child. I am That. I am a Tantric Master that has both forms of Consciousness fully integrating in the body and living it. I come from beyond the beyond. I belong to beyond the beyond as you also belong only to this.

To find out more about B Prior's
teaching and events worldwide, go to:

www.bprior.org

or contact:

B Prior Foundation
30 Teddington Rd
Governors Bay 8971

info@bernieprior.org
+64 3 3299 288